Conflict Management

&

Conflict Resolution

in Corrections

Thomas F. Christian, Ph.D.

FOUNDED 1870
American Correctional Association
Lanham, Maryland

American Correctional Association Staff

Richard L. Stalder, President
James A. Gondles, Jr., Executive Director
Gabriella M. Daley, Director, Communications and Publications
Leslie A. Maxam, Assistant Director, Communications and Publications
Alice Fins, Publications Managing Editor
Michael Kelly, Associate Editor
Sherry Wulfekuhle, Editorial Assistant

Cover and layout by Capitol Communication Systems, Inc.

Printed in the United States of America by Versa Press, Inc., Illinois
For information on publications and videos available from ACA, contact our worldwide web home page at: http://www.corrections.com/aca

ISBN 978-1-56991-096-2 (pbk.)

This publication may be ordered from:
American Correctional Association
206 N. Washington Street, Suite 200
Alexandria, VA 22314
800-222-5646

Library of Congress Cataloging-in-Publications Data
Christian, Thomas F.
 Conflict management and conflict resolution in corrections / Thomas F. Christian.
  p. cm.
 ISBN 1-56991-096-0 (pbk.)
 1. Corrections. 2. Conflict management. 3. Correctional personnel—Job stress.
I. Title.
HV8763.C54 1998
365'.068'4—dc21   98-50580
                                                                   CIP

conflict continues while the justice system supervises the offender. The correctional professional needs tools to manage and resolve these difficult, everyday conflicts to be effective in helping coworkers and clients manage and resolve their own conflict situations. With the proper skills, correctional professionals can handle crisis situations, manage everyday conflicts, and often resolve complex problems. They also can teach others these techniques and together build a safer work environment while creating a better community on the job, at home, and in society.

Conflict

Conflict is normal. It is okay to see things differently from the person next to you. How you handle a given situation is the key to conflict management and conflict resolution. Conflict can create an opportunity to learn, or it can produce aggravation, frustration, and unnecessary trouble. It can lead to an ongoing uncomfortable and even dangerous living and working environment. Individuals should not simply react to conflict; they should view conflict as a situation that has to be managed and, if possible, resolved. If people manage conflict and resolve their problems, life can go on rather smoothly. If not, matters can escalate, fester, and ultimately cause major damage to individuals and relationships, and in a correctional climate they can end in violence, riots, or other tragedies. And in today's society, there is the inevitable lawsuit.

People have different perceptions of events based on family, genes, peers, relationships, values, community, education, religion, life experiences, culture, exposure to the media, and a number of other variables. Two heads are normally better than one. If two individuals share their perceptions on a given situation, both can benefit. If one chooses to block out any other opinion or option, conflict can surface.

Conflict comes from two words, *con* (together) and *fligere* (to strike). If two people are in conflict and beat each other down, both will lose. If two people focus together on the problem, both can win. The secret in conflict management is to "strike together" on the *problem*—not the person.

In a correctional environment, the tendency is to view things in an *adversary* mode. It is "us against them." This can mean the inmate, probationer, or parolee, but it also can roll over to other staff, the administration, family, visitors, and the public, in general. For example, the inmates can see the correctional officer as the "screw" whose job it is to keep constant pressure on the inmates to make their lives miserable and to keep them in line. In turn, the correctional officer can view the inmate as someone who always is trying to get over on the staff, and thus it becomes a game of who can win and beat the other person at his or her own game. Correctional officers can see themselves as the keepers and the inmates as the ones who are kept. Or, the correctional officers can see themselves as the persons who have to manage difficult relationships, keep order, and teach responsibility and accountability. Probation officers can see themselves as the ones who must conduct surveillance and threaten revocation or as persons who have to manage an individual in a community setting and use every resource available to teach responsibility and accountability. To portray a person who is looking for cooperation and mutual respect rather than disrespect or confrontation is the difference between creating an adversarial atmosphere and a conflict-management mode.

Effectively managing conflict and resolving problems can create a better work environment, and it is a tool for all phases of life. It has the potential not only to make a person a more skilled worker, but it also has the power to help that person become a happier individual. Happier people make better family members, compatible neighbors, and more productive workers. The world needs more conflict managers and problem resolvers. The field of corrections is in a position to make a difference. The people with the conflicts in the justice system can learn how to manage conflict and resolve problems or continue to act out against society. If correctional professionals are to help the people they interact with, they must exercise the skills of effective conflict managers in all phases of their lives.

Crime and the Overburdened Criminal Justice System

Crime in our society is a complex problem that has no easy answers. As violence escalates, the criminal justice system becomes more and more overburdened. Communities are fearful and victims are vulnerable. Offenders repeat their crimes because the punishment from the criminal justice system does not change their behavior. The police are frustrated, the courts are congested and have limited options, the probation caseloads are high, and the detention facilities and prisons are crowded and expensive, while people on parole too often do not adjust and are back in prison in a matter of months after release. To say that managing crime and its aftermath is a challenging task is an understatement.

Crime is really a lack of conflict management, and it is the consequence of a failure to resolve problems. Half of crime, including homicides, is between people who know each other (Bureau of Justice Statistics, Criminal Victimization in the United States, 1994). Family, relatives, neighbors, friends, and coworkers have disagreements that can lead to a violation of the law. Therefore, many incidents called crime are really interpersonal relationships gone wrong. Even stranger-upon-stranger crime often involves a lack of managing one's life. Loss of control through drugs, coupled with immature responses to conflict situations, and a lack of power to handle everyday responsibilities, create negative reactions. If people knew how to manage conflict situations, crime potentially could be reduced.

Teaching young people in school conflict-management and conflict-resolution skills can prepare the next generation to have respect for each other and life, in general. The fourth "r" should be the resolution of conflicts to go along with reading, 'riting, and 'rithmetic. Talking out a problem together is a lot better than acting out that anger, which results in tragic consequences. Behavior is learned, and parents are the number one teachers, especially in the key first three years of life.

Conflict resolution skills should be taught in every juvenile offender facility. If youthful offenders can learn how to manage conflict situations, violence and drug use has the potential to be reduced. Conflict-management skills can replace drugs (avoidance) and violence (confrontation) as answers for life's problems.

If a portion of crime is due to mismanagement of conflict, this matter can be addressed with the present resources through teachers and correctional professionals. Not only should we teach conflict management and conflict resolution as part of the curriculum in school, but we also should include it in parenting classes, seminars for probationers and parolees, in classes taught in detention facilities (jails), and in both juvenile and adult correctional facilities. Teaching new parents conflict resolution skills allows them to be role models for their children and each other.

If police, probation officers, community-based program staff, detention and correctional officers, and parole agents are all trained conflict managers, skills can be reinforced with every conflict opportunity, and life can be a little more peaceful for everyone involved. For example, Nate Carter burglarized the building where he had been employed. Obviously, he had a conflict with his employer who had let him go. This was a great opportunity for his probation officer, Bill Sinclair, to intervene before or even after Nate was fired and mediate between Nate and his employer.

During this conflict resolution process, Bill Sinclair is not advocating for his probationer, and he is not on the employer's side. He is a neutral party who is trying to help both people communicate and find out what problems can be identified and addressed. This process could have prevented the burglary, maybe saved Nate's job, and potentially taught Nate how to deal with conflict in a constructive way. In turn, the employer would not have had to hire and train a new employee.

Cindy Hughes struggles with her daughter, Lily, and could benefit from a parent-child mediation. This process could be handled by her probation officer, Joyce Hennessey, and does not have to threaten Cindy's parental authority but would give Lily the feeling that she can work out her problems with her mother without her mother feeling that she is a rebellious teenager who needs intense counseling.

Victims

Victims are the result of conflict that was not managed well. All people suffer when a situation arises that is not constructively discussed, identified, and either managed or resolved. In a family or work environment, conflict is intertwined and can strangle the parties. It can cut off valuable opportunities to communicate, appreciate, and even enjoy each other. The situation can be complicated further if a problem is medicated through alcohol or other drugs because while under these substances, the person cannot function effectively. If the interaction cannot be managed consistently, the problem will continue to grow out of control. In that case, responsibilities will be avoided and relationships will be devastated. If victims can experience positive, managed interventions, then problems—not people—can be attacked, and victims can be empowered rather than revictimized. Positive relationships can be made better through communication, reparation, and closure. Conflict management and conflict resolution are key to all relationships and necessary for helping every past, present, and future victim.

Recidivism

When someone does something wrong, gets caught, and nonetheless does it again, it usually is a sign of immaturity. People learn from their mistakes, and they learn from their behavior. If the role model—whether a parent or criminal justice professional—teaches the offender how to handle conflict constructively, the likelihood of the offender repeating the negative behavior diminishes. The offender thinks about the behavior, the choices that were made, and the results and consequences of those choices.

For example, Cindy Hughes was convicted of passing bad checks. She proceeded to go out and "hang bad paper" again shortly after her sentence to probation. Joyce Hennessey, her probation officer, could have sat her down with the first victim and conducted a mediation to help Cindy see the consequences of her behavior. The probation officer could have drawn up a restitution agreement and a reasonable payment schedule. With such mediation, Cindy may have seen the results of her crime on the victim and with gainful employment, concentrated on repaying the victim rather than recommitting the same offense.

In constructive conflict management, the focus is on the opportunity to learn rather than the mistake. Repetition is the mother of all learning. Therefore, people who repeat certain behavior should learn right from wrong unless the system puts the emphasis on the behavior and punishment instead of the educational value of the situation. Recidivism should be an opportunity to learn new behaviors rather than just an opportunity to punish. If offenders have positive relationships with correctional professionals, they can begin to relate better with family, friends, and society. With better relationships comes more thoughtful behavior and less violence.

Conflicting Models

The criminal justice system has presented a number of conflicting models over the years. There always has been an emphasis on punishment.

- **Retributive justice** is the just deserts approach. If you do the crime, then do the time. The punishment is a consequence for committing an act that is not allowed in society. The punishment can range from limiting one's freedom with supervision in the community under certain conditions (for example, probation) to the loss of freedom through incarceration in a correctional institution (jail or prison). The person is expected to learn from the punishment and not do the crime again.

- The **deterrence** model is based on the assumption that average people do not commit crimes because they do not want to be caught and suffer the humiliation and problems that are the result of being processed through the justice system. If people are punished through probation supervision or incarceration, they will learn from the experience and not repeat the crime.

- The **incapacitation** model takes the perpetrator out of circulation for a period of time through incarceration. It protects the community and prevents that person from committing new crimes on the streets. The majority of people, however, eventually are released back to their communities.

- **Rehabilitation** is a model that tries to meet the needs of the person in trouble with the law. Education, drug treatment, counseling, and employment assistance are possible limitations that have to be addressed to help the offenders change their negative behavior.

- The **reintegration** model centers on working the individual who has been incarcerated back into being a productive member of society through parole and/or a community program, such as a halfway house.

- The **restorative justice** model requires offenders to be held accountable for their actions and to make efforts to repair the harm through restitution to the victim, the victim's family, and the community. An opportunity to see the consequences for one's behavior and to express remorse is available. The victim can gain a sense of peace through receiving information and a feeling of closure. The community benefits through community service and an involved victim. Punishment alone is not enough. All the key actors must make an effort to right the wrong.

Conflicting models can create a frustrating work environment and a confused correctional professional. If a correctional professional takes one approach (for example, punishment) and the next correctional professional takes another (for example, rehabilitation), then there will be ongoing conflict in the justice system. Is the intent of the corrections field to correct or only to punish? Should the punishment be supervision, incarceration, and the loss of freedom? If the intent is to correct, then the role of the correctional personnel should be to teach the lawbreaker how to manage problems in life; the role should not be to continue punishing the individual everyday through demands, intimidation, and other demeaning treatment.

Sol Wachtler, the former Chief Judge of the State of New York, explained how disappointed and dismayed he was over the way he was treated by correctional personnel during his fifteen-month incarceration for harassing the woman with whom he had an adulterous affair. He estimated that the majority of the staff gave the impression that it was their role not only to incapacitate him but to humiliate and intimidate him and to continue punishing him at every possible opportunity. That left only a minority of the staff who treated him as a human being.

Yes, he had done something wrong and was being punished with the loss of his freedom. That he was prepared to accept. But to be punished over and over again by professional correctional staff was devastating.

Jim Bakker, the televangelist who was convicted of defrauding his followers, stated that he had the same experience while he was incarcerated. He was so harassed by the correctional staff that the deputy superintendent worried that he would commit suicide.

There are many dedicated, caring correctional professionals in facilities, probation, and parole, but the experience of Sol Wachtler and Jim Bakker unfortunately is repeated day after day and considered part of the job. When an "ordinary" inmate expresses the same feelings, the public does not have a lot of sympathy for them. After having worked in the corrections environment over the past thirty-five years, this author would reluctantly have to agree with Judge Wachtler and Reverend Bakker. This tendency to see one's role as part of the punishment is not good conflict management.

On the other hand, there are dedicated correctional staff who are ready to go the extra mile. In one case, a correctional officer noticed that one inmate's visitor was not picked up for her ride back to her community. The visitor had paid forty dollars to have someone take her to and from the institution. After the officer notified the inmate of his visitor's problem, the inmate tried to call for someone to pick her up. When no one could be located late in the day, the correctional officer drove her to the bus station and bought her a ticket. On the next visit, he refused to be repaid. The word went out throughout the prison population that this correctional officer (a sergeant) cared. From that act and others, he always received cooperation and respect from the inmates.

We as correctional professionals have to look at our role in the justice system seriously. Corrections must have clear goals and objectives. Conflict management and conflict resolution techniques can play a major role in consistency and in achieving positive results that can benefit the correctional staff, the inmate, the probationer, the parolee, and the public we serve. The goal is to restore a sense of justice to the victim, the offender, and the community, and this goal should be at the forefront of every correctional professional's credo. The tools to accomplish this are available.

Conflicting Expectations

There are conflicting expectations from the public, the police, the courts, and corrections. The public and communities want safe streets, but does that mean locking up all perpetrators of all ages for longer and longer periods of time? The police want the handcuffs taken off of them so they can do their job, but abuse of power and authority is always a reality, and today such evidence of abuse also is available on videotape. (The author's grandfather, father, and brother were law enforcement officers for three generations, so he understands the frustrations of the peace officer and has the highest respect for good professional police work.)

Judges must provide a fair trial for all citizens who are innocent until proven guilty beyond a reasonable doubt. If convicted, the court must sentence the offender, but limited options and resources leave the judges with two basic alternatives—probation or prison. Probation and community-based corrections programs are hampered by restricted resources and limited capacity. As a probation officer, the author had such a large caseload that he was lucky to remember his assigned people by name. He had to broker them out to programs and volunteers. Creative judges, however, can look for resources, demand more options, and make the penalty fit the crime so the victim, the offender, and the community are repaired, and justice is restored rather than just punishment being meted out. For example, a referral by the judge to mediation for appropriate cases will allow the people to talk to each other with a trained mediator under the court's supervision, find out the reasons for the behavior, and determine restitution and future conditions that must be met.

Correctional facilities are told not to just warehouse inmates but to provide educational opportunities, counseling, and industry to prepare people to return to their communities. At the same time, corrections is told not to create a "country club" atmosphere. In the many prisons where this writer has worked or that he has visited, none comes close to anything resembling a country club. The expectations in and about the criminal justice system are unrealistic and conflicting at all levels.

Conflicting Responses

There seemingly are conflicting responses to all of these issues. The communities can provide programs for offenders or hand off these responsibilities to others and wash their hands of criminals until they come back into their neighborhoods. Yet, corrections is everyone's business. The majority of offenders—except those with life with no possibility of parole—will come out of prison sooner or later, and they will return to our communities. Instead of incarcerating over a million citizens, perhaps it is time to create a balance by incarcerating dangerous people and individuals out of control while developing more community programs with effective supervision for other offenders. The conflict management and conflict resolution needs of the correctional facility—both inmates and staff—would be served better and be under more control if the population were smaller rather than crowded and volatile. If this occurred, more programs could be afforded and made available in the institutions, and rather than warehousing people, in-depth work could be done with inmates who are in need and ready to address their behavior.

The police can continue to arrest parties and send them further up the system or balance their approach and feature community policing to help people manage conflict, solve problems, and direct parties to community resources thereby preventing and reducing crime. Community dispute resolution centers now are available in every state to serve the justice system. Many cases can be diverted to these centers where the people themselves can talk to each other rather than at each other, identify their problems, and work out acceptable solutions under the assistance of trained, experienced mediators.

Judges can sentence people to community restitution and demand more resources for community supervision, particularly in the area of drug use and abuse. Drug courts are a prime example. The adversarial approach leaves the focus on punishing the person rather than resolving the individual's problem, which is frequently a combination of drug use, unemployment, educational limitations, negative attitudes and relationships, and/or poverty. People choose their behavior; but with conflict-management skills, they can identify the problem, make better choices, and resolve their difficulties rather than have their problems escalate into serious criminal matters. Relationships will improve, and people will care more about what their behavior does to others in their communities. Violence can be reduced. In the case of Cindy Hughes and her sixteen-year-old daughter, Lilly, the probation officer, Joyce Hennessey, could sit the mother and daughter down together and help them communicate with each other. Together, they can identify the problems, clarify the issues, and make choices that they both can live with in the future. For Cindy, to do nothing gives her daughter free reign. On the other hand, to slap her daughter around out of frustration teaches her daughter that violence is the answer, and her daughter can turn physically on her mother or strike out at her peers, turn to drugs, and maybe attempt suicide to get away from it all.

To address society's problems, the justice system needs a comprehensive, consistent response through the community, law enforcement, the courts, and corrections. Constructive conflict-management and conflict-resolution methods are essential for a positive and effective response.

Table of Contents

Foreword

A survey conducted by ACA for our publication, *Use of Force: Current Practice and Policy*, revealed that nearly all correctional systems engage in conflict resolution. Thus, it is important to know what conflict resolution and management entails and how it fits into the framework of a restorative justice approach. Thomas Christian's book provides an explanation of how to handle conflict with positive results for all disputants. He explains why this approach is important for both inmates and staff, and for the relationship between them.

Using conflict resolution in a correctional setting makes sense. It can lower the tension among all parties involved and can help the disputants understand that there are alternatives in making decisions other than using aggression or force. Such an approach has repercussions, which may lead to lower recidivism and greater management ease in facilities and in the community.

The author has had a long career in many areas of corrections, so he understands the realities of prisons, jails, and community corrections. He speaks to the reader in an easy-to-understand style and employs examples that are based on his noteworthy experiences.

We welcome reader feedback on this publication. Please contact us at our website: www.aca.org, or write us at 206 N. Washington Street, Suite 200, Alexandria, VA 22314.

James A. Gondles, Jr.
Executive Director
American Correctional Association

Preface

This is a work that is based on the author's experience in conflict management and conflict resolution in the justice system over the past thirty-five years. He hopes that it is not one year's experience repeated thirty-five times. It is written from one person's point of view, and if it can be helpful to you, whatever your role is, then it will serve its purpose. This is not a Ph.D. dissertation. That was accomplished by this writer back in 1973 for another purpose and at another time. This also is not an effort to write the last word on conflict management and conflict resolution. It simply is sharing what has worked for one professional in a career dedicated to people in the field of criminal justice.

Tom Christian has experience in correctional facilities (prisons), detention facilities (jails), has served as a senior probation officer, and has run community-based corrections programs. The author also served as the State Director of the Minnesota International Halfway House Association and as the State Director of the Minnesota Community Corrections Association. Here, he was voted by the Minnesota Corrections Association as the Corrections Person of the Year (1979) and given the Professional Achievement Award by the Minnesota Community Corrections Association.

Additionally, Dr. Christian has worked extensively in four states (Minnesota, Michigan, Georgia, and New York) and has provided technical assistance in twenty other states and in a number of foreign countries. In his last position, he was the State Director of the Community Dispute Resolution Centers Program for the New York State Unified Court System. In this role, he served people in civil, family, and criminal conflicts from misdemeanor matters and restitution to victim and offender mediations for serious felonies. After fifteen years there, he took an early retirement to have time to write and do some training based on those years of experience. He was encouraged from others in the field of criminal justice to write down ideas on conflict management, conflict resolution, and restorative justice, and the result is this present work. These preliminary comments should assist the reader in knowing where the author is coming from and where he has been.

Take what is said in this book for whatever it is worth to you. We expect that you will not agree with everything you read here. That is okay. It may be a difference of opinion and experience. It is a form of conflict, but conflict can be an opportunity to learn. All we ask is that you listen to what this correctional professional has to say and think about some of the concepts and ideas; then, use whatever may be helpful to you in your conflict experiences. If the reader gains one idea, this work will have been worth the effort.

The good news in corrections is that the criminal justice system is improving now that there are more women and people of color working in the field. This infusion of diverse correctional professionals means that staff and offenders can see firsthand how people from various backgrounds and with different perceptions can work together, overcome conflict, and help one another.

In this volume, we use the term "inmate" for the person who is incarcerated in a correctional or detention facility. We considered using the term client, resident, or perpetrator, but the word inmate really means a "mate who is in." Just as someone from Australia or a sailor would use the term on a friendly basis, this author prefers the term "inmate" because the people incarcerated are human beings who have committed acts that have placed them in these circumstances. They, therefore, are our mates who happen to be "in" at the present time.

We are against criminal behavior, but we still must respect all individuals as persons. Inmates do not have to earn our respect for their humanity. We want them to choose to change the actions that have hurt themselves, others, and the community. The fact that society has taken away their liberty because of their actions does not mean they have lost their basic dignity and the right to be treated as human beings.

The author's grandfather, father, and brothers have been in law enforcement. His grandfather, William George Carney, died as a result of injuries in the line of duty. His father, Edward Howard Christian, who was two months from retirement from a lifetime career on the police department, was getting ready to go to work in the squad car on the eight-to-four shift when he had a cerebral hemorrhage and died. His brother, Ken Christian, recently retired after working in the field of criminal justice for forty-four years. Enjoy walking in the forest, Ken. Also, his brother, Ed, has been an attorney handling criminal, civil, and family cases for thirty-four years. As the family often jokingly says, "we have nothing economically against crime—our family has depended on it for generations."

On the other hand, this writer's uncle, Chester Carney, spent eight-and-one-half years in a correctional facility for highjacking a whiskey truck. He was an alcoholic and after he was released, he dedicated the rest of his life to helping other alcoholics by doing twelve-step and detoxification work. He tried to repair the damage he had caused himself and his community. He was an "inmate," but he also reached out to his mates who were dependent on alcohol and other drugs. A first cousin of the author also served a three-year sentence for burglary and a ten-year sentence in a Mexican prison for attempting to buy marijuana to sell to his friends. Since then, he has been working constructively in his community for more than twenty years.

These personal matters are shared with you, the reader, so that you will know why this author respects people who dedicate their life to the justice field, and also, why he views offenders as people who have to take responsibility for their behavior and begin to repair the damage their acts have caused. Offenders are human beings and deserve to be treated as members of the human family. Criminal justice professionals and criminal offenders both literally come from the author's immediate family.

You were warned that you might not agree with all that is proposed in this book, so if you feel this approach is not your approach, then just look at how you manage and resolve conflict. If you are comfortable with your approach, then keep growing by listening and gaining knowledge from everyone you talk to and interact with in life. If you think your conflict management and resolution style has not been altogether effective or if you are not comfortable with the way you handle conflict situations, maybe the ideas presented here can be helpful.

There are two themes that run throughout this book. The first is that all correctional professionals need a set of tools to manage and resolve conflicts in the criminal justice field. The second theme is that these tools must be used not just to manage and resolve conflicts, but also to build a positive, constructive community and working environment. Just as law enforcement officers can use community policing as a problem-solving tool to better their community, the correctional professionals can see the cellblock and the probation or parole caseload as their working neighborhood and community. They can make the neighborhood a better place to work and live for coworkers, clients, and families.

Thank you for taking the time to read this preface. It is important for understanding this work.

Acknowledgments

I would like to thank the following people for their help in putting together the ideas for this book: my wife, Bernice; my sons, Craig and Andy; my daughter Jen; and my brothers Ken, Ed, Dave (deceased), and Mike; my former New York State dispute resolution staff: Mark Collins, Yvonne Taylor, Tom Buckner, and especially Jeremy Kropp for his editing assistance; Ellen Donovan for her search of the existing literature; Howard Zehr, Mark Umbreit, and Dennis Wittman for their dialog and sharing over the years on restorative justice and victim and offender mediation; Wayne Blanchard, Gary Geiger, William J. Kreidler, Ruf North, and Michael Quinn for their ideas on conflict management; Alice Fins and her staff at the American Correctional Association, and all the correctional personnel, victims, and correctional clients I have worked with over the past thirty-five years. I have listened and gained helpful knowledge from each of them.

Dedication

This work is dedicated to my late parents Ruth Leone Carney and Officer Edward Howard Christian, who taught me that conflict can be managed—and usually resolved—if we work at it as members of one human family.

Terms and Vocabulary

Correctional Professional

Throughout this book, the title "correctional professional" describes all personnel who work in federal, state, and local correctional facilities—namely prisons and detention areas (jails), probation offices, parole agencies, and community-based corrections programs. This includes people on all levels from administration to line staff. All are responsible for managing and resolving conflicts.

Inmate

For reasons discussed in the Preface, the author uses the term "inmate" (a mate who is in) to describe prisoners in a federal, state, or local correctional facility and for detainees in jail.

Probationer/Parolee

The author defines probationers as those individuals sentenced by the court to community supervision and defines those people under community supervision who have served a portion of their prison term as parolees.

Community Corrections

Any program outside a correctional institution comes under the category of community corrections. Probationers and parolees participate in community corrections. Residents are those individuals in community-based correctional residential facilities, such as halfway houses and treatment centers. Programs that have people come during the day or evening for activities—such as pretrial diversion programs, employment counseling, school activities, and so forth—are included in this category.

Offender/Client/Perpetrator

The term "offender" describes a person who has been convicted of a crime and is either under community supervision or incarcerated in a correctional facility. They have "offended" people in their community. If an offender is involved in a specific treatment program, he or she is referred to as a client. The term "perpetrators" refers to persons who have committed a crime against themselves or other members of their community.

Chapter I

Introduction to Conflict*

Nathaniel Carter: A Case Study

Nathaniel "Nate" Carter was convicted of burglarizing a building where he had been employed for three weeks. He was retaliating for being fired earlier that day. He has an extensive juvenile record, and this burglary offense was his second adult-felony conviction.

Nate had quit school at the age of sixteen because he said his teachers made fun of him. His peers teased him for his strange, alternative lifestyle and excluded him from their activities. Nate found solace in a loosely formed gang of like-minded people who dressed the way he did and listened to the same music. He drank, smoked dope, and used whatever he could get ahold of to escape his sense of isolation and cope with his feelings of despair. The establishment viewed him as a "loser."

Nate's parents had gone through a divorce and both stated that they could not handle him. He was on his own and lived with whomever would put up with him. He had beaten up his girlfriend, Tina Lopez, on more than one occasion, despite her loyalty to him even after his broken promises to stop drinking and taking drugs. Before his arrest for the burglary and while he was on probation for a previous crime, Nate lied to his probation officer, Bill Sinclair, who did little to challenge Nate's fantastic excuses for missing his probation meetings. If Nate wanted to fail on probation, Bill saw this as Nate's choice.

Judge Lawrence A. Lawson sentenced Nate to one-to-three years in prison for the burglary. He physically fought with the police after he was arrested. He claimed that he was the victim of police brutality. In jail, he had frequent run-ins with the deputy sheriffs. He did not cooperate with

---

*Case studies in this publication are composites of several individuals who have been given fictitious names.

his assigned counsel, Nancy Wilcox, and in court, he informed Judge Lawson that he did not care what type of sentence he was given. In prison, he mouthed off to the correctional officers, made no effort to communicate with the correctional counselor, Mark Linderman, and slept in his school classes. After he served his prison term, he was assigned to a parole agent, Brenda Williams, who was frustrated by his lack of direction and failure to change.

Cynthia Leslie Hughes: A Case Study

Cynthia "Cindy" Leslie Hughes is a thirty-four-year-old woman convicted over the past sixteen years of passing bad checks, illegally using credit cards, and possession of stolen property. She was in constant conflict with her teenage daughter, Lily, and slapped her around so much that protective services has threatened to take her daughter away from her. She buys drugs for her boyfriend, accuses the police of racism when they are called to her home, avoids her probation officer, Joyce Hennessey, and is depressed over her lot in life. She had done up to a year in the local detention facility. She had a major attitude problem with the sheriff's department and the deputies while in jail. She has threatened to sue over alleged mistreatment by correctional officer Gail Overland.

Analysis of Case Studies

Nate and Cindy are classic examples of people out of control and in need of managing the conflict in their lives and resolving many of the problems they face each day. If they do not learn how to control themselves, they likely will continue as recidivists. The correctional professionals who encounter Nate Carter and Cindy Hughes have opportunities either to teach them how to manage conflict in their lives and resolve many of the problems that have landed them in their present predicament or to make a sincere initial effort and then pass them on to another part of the justice system. We will follow the cases of Nate and Cindy and the people they interact with in the justice system through our discussion of conflict management and conflict resolution in corrections.

Conflict management and conflict resolution are major challenges for everyone working in the field of corrections. Conflict has brought clients like Nate Carter and Cindy Hughes into the justice system. Whether conflict is aggravated by mental problems, different values, or drugs—or if it is the result of stressful relationships or a lack of meaningful relationships—this

Chapter II

Techniques and Tools for Conflict Management in Corrections

There are a number of ways to manage conflict in any given situation. Each approach may be successful depending on the circumstances and the individuals involved. An effective conflict manager will have a number of responses or tools ready to apply when the occasion arises. The style that is used most often, however, will determine the true effectiveness of the correctional conflict manager. If the primary approach is cooperative and collaborative, the conflict manager will be the most effective person at home, in the neighborhood, and on the job.

Just as a skilled craftsperson needs a number of tools to be effective, so too does a good conflict manager. Knowing how and when to use the correct instrument is essential. What are the techniques that a conflict manager must have to function in problem situations?

Avoidance

Avoidance is the most frequently used approach in conflict situations. It is also one of the worst ways to deal with an issue.

In the case study of Nathaniel Carter, Nate uses avoidance by not communicating with his employer; quitting school; withdrawing from his parents, teachers, and peers; and escaping into drugs. Also, Nate avoids difficult situations by not cooperating with his probation officer, Bill Sinclair, his assigned counsel, Nancy Wilcox, and his correctional counselor, Bill Linderman.

Similarly, Nate's employer, teachers, parents, attorney, correctional counselor, and parole agent all avoided addressing Nate and his difficulties. They concluded that he was not ready to change and wrote him off as a loser. With conflict-management training, they might have been able to gain his trust and cooperation.

In Cynthia Leslie Hughes' case, Cindy avoids her probation officer, Joyce Hennessey, and turns her anger in on herself creating her depression. She avoids responsibility and blames others for her plight. It is her daughter Lily's fault, the police are racist, and the jail correctional officer, Gail Overland, was too rough. Yet, Cynthia Leslie Hughes enables her boyfriend to use drugs and takes no responsibility for her own behavior. The tendency for correctional professionals is to see her as weak, and they, too, avoid making her accountable. Therefore, nothing is done, nothing changes, and she sinks deeper into the criminal justice system.

Is it always wrong for a person to employ avoidance methods? No. However, it is the equivalent of doing nothing. Sometimes it is best to leave well enough alone; not addressing the issue often does cause the problem simply to go away. Withdrawing from the situation gives everybody the opportunity to cool down, think about the circumstances, and perhaps develop a better tactic. If a person is very upset and on the verge of going out of control, the avoidance method may be the answer.

To just stand there and not aggravate the individual may have a calming effect. The person knows you are there, and you are respecting his or her feelings. To escalate the situation may cause the matter to get out of hand. To simply have a presence may be all that is needed. If a staff person is upset over a work matter, perhaps a good listener will serve as a sounding board. Remember, listen (LISTEN) uses the same letters as silent (SILENT). If one is truly listening, that person should be silent. If angry individuals are allowed to vent constructively, they might feel better and the problems may solve themselves.

If a family member, coworker, friend, or client is not in the mood to deal with a given situation, it may be better to postpone the matter for a later date. Correctional officers do not have to be in a hurry. The inmate is serving time and is not going anywhere. If the correctional officers see every conflict situation as an opportunity to teach the inmates how to handle a problem rather than as a challenge to their authority, the inmates will sense the difference and respond accordingly. If the inmates do not respond constructively, the correctional officers can move into another conflict-management strategy. The person who uses avoidance correctly and sparingly gives everybody the time to see things more clearly and with a calmer manner.

A man married eighty years was asked the secret formula for his long, successful married life. He said that when his wife was angry, he would shut up and listen and they would work it out together later when emotions were not so sensitive. He and his wife both smiled when he gave this sage advice. Avoidance used at the proper time and the proper place can be the answer to a number of conflict situations. As a style of conflict management, it should be used only as an auxiliary method. If the problem eventually has to be faced, do so as soon as possible. It is better than being too late.

An example of doing nothing that can be harmful to all is the case of the cell with the stuffed-up toilet. If the correctional professional does nothing in an effort to "teach the inmate a lesson and let him sit in his own mess," the whole cellblock can be affected by the stench and potential for disease. The inmate is upset and focuses on the fact that he is not given any consideration, and he holds the correctional officer responsible for not doing anything. If the inmate did it on purpose, he should be held accountable for his actions and not punished by the staff who do nothing.

Another negative example of avoidance is the new young inmate who is being bothered by the older inmate as a possible sexual partner. If nothing is done by the correctional officer, the inmate is in more danger of being attacked. Action taken by the officer can communicate awareness and concern for the inmate and the living environment. Inaction is an indication that the correctional officer sees this situation as the inmate's inability to adjust to the reality of living in a same-sex prison.

A person who avoids literally does nothing. In a negative way, one can avoid an event by ignoring the other person or by walking away from the situation. Looking straight through persons as if they were not there is one example of this behavior. Usually the problem either escalates or the individuals are frustrated and reinforced in their frustration for the next encounter. Sometimes avoidance is an answer to a pesky inmate who just wants attention.

Normally, avoidance is not a good solution because the issues are not addressed. If inmates think that nothing is being done, they may be frustrated and see inaction as business as usual. The conflict manager explains to the inmates that at the present time what can be done is being done. A correctional professional who avoids responsibility is contributing to the problem rather than solving it. Avoidance should be used when it is effective until the correctional professional can employ a cooperative and collaborative approach.

Accommodation

Accommodating is known as soft bargaining or killing the other person with kindness. Yielding to the other persons' point of view and paying attention to their concerns often neglects one's own needs. To admit that one is wrong, but not believe it, will not resolve anything. This strategy may be effective temporarily in developing a relationship, but can be devastating if used as a major conflict-management technique in a correctional environment. To give in always can get tiring in a hurry.

In Nate's case, his relationship with his girlfriend is one of accommodation. She enabled him to use drugs and always agreed with his excuses. The resentment ultimately erupted into violent arguments. Also, probation officer Bill Sinclair's unwillingness to challenge Nate when Nate lied to him facilitated Nate's recidivism. Similarly, Cindy Hughes also solves her dilemmas by accommodating her boyfriend and purchasing drugs for him to buy his companionship.

To pretend to agree can be dishonest at best and can lead to resentment and a build up of anger. On the other hand, if people are accommodating, it often causes the other parties to rethink their approach, and all can benefit from this experience. A good approach is to put oneself in the other person's place and ask how the reversal of roles would affect the same scenario. Again, the secret is to use accommodation when it can be effective and not adopt it as the main conflict strategy.

A good use of an accommodating style of conflict management in corrections can involve a probation officer who agrees to change an office visit so the probationer can make babysitting arrangements. To avoid manipulation, the probation officer can talk the situation over with the probationer on the next visit and show a willingness to help the probationer solve her own problems. In the best of worlds, the probationer mirrors the probation officer's accommodating behavior and tries harder to cooperate and benefit from the advice and example.

An example of the wrong use of accommodating conflict management would be to allow the probationer to develop a pattern of last minute changes to a point where she has to be returned to court for not reporting on a timely basis.

In a correctional setting, a good use of accommodating behavior is to assist an inmate's visitors by making sure that there are enough chairs for each family member. The inmate and family see this effort and respond with a cooperative attitude and the visit runs smoothly for the correctional staff and inmate alike. In the same scenario, a poor use of accommodation is for the correctional officer to smile and laugh and allow the inmate's visitors to become too boisterous and cause another supervising officer to intervene and tone down the activity. Accommodating others for the right reason and for the desired effect can be a powerful tool in working with people and managing conflict.

Compromise

Compromise is not a bad thing. People do not necessarily compromise their position by splitting the difference, nor do individuals compromise their values if they seek middle ground. Compromise means to "promise together." If one side gives in a little, it may encourage the other side to do the same.

On the other hand, in the famous story in the Bible, King Solomon had a dilemma when two new mothers stood before him and asked him to solve their problem. During the night, one of the infants had died. The one mother whose baby had died realized that her baby was dead and, while the other mother slept, changed the babies. When the second mother awoke to nurse her child, she saw it was dead and, looking closely, realized it was not her infant. Both claimed to be the mother of the living child. King Solomon's solution was to cut the living child and the dead infant in two, giving half to each mother. The story continues with the real mother saying, "no" and giving up her child to the other mother. The mother of the dead child agrees with the King's solution. The end of the story has the King give the living child to the rightful mother because she gave the right answer as the true mother. So, compromise may not be the best answer if the end result is worse than the original conflict.

Again, the use of compromise in appropriate situations may be the best answer. To use compromise as the major tool in dealing with conflict is too limiting and often leaves both sides unsatisfied. Both parties win something, but both individuals also lose something. Often, it is better to have both sides talk to each other and negotiate rather than simply splitting the problem in two.

An example of a good compromise is used by the parole officer, Brenda Williams, who works out an arrangement with parolee Nate Carter to reduce his office visits to once a month as long as he maintains employment. If he loses or quits his job, then he must again report weekly. A poor use of compromise occurs when a correctional officer agrees not to report a coworker who steals packages of food from the prison kitchen as long as the coworker provides him with a share of the supplies.

Confrontation

Confrontation or competition is second only to avoidance in how frequently it is used in conflict situations. Like avoidance, it is also one of the worst ways to deal with conflict. In the field of corrections, unfortunately, it is the method often adopted by staff to show power and express authority, perhaps out of a fear that inmates will run the institution if correctional professionals fail immediately to establish who is in charge.

Good conflict management requires the staff and inmate population to work together to run the facility efficiently. To do this, all parties need to be skilled in conflict-management expertise. This requires training and a commitment from all sides.

Competing with an inmate who has mastered taking advantage of the establishment is no small challenge. It can be intimidating, to say the least. If the mentality is "us against them," the adversarial approach wins out again. If it is a matter of competition, there are no real winners in the correctional arena. Inmates usually have the last say because they can make life difficult and frustrating for staff. In turn, the staff reciprocates and the battle never ends.

Nate Carter's confrontational style left him in trouble with the police at the time of his arrest, the judge at the time of his sentencing, and the correctional officers when he talked back to them. His answer to problems with his girlfriend, Tina Lopez, was violence. The deputy sheriffs in the jail and the correctional officers in the prison escalated difficult situations by responding to Nate's hostility with more confrontation. Cindy Hughes confronts the police with accusations of racism and the correctional officer, Gail Overland, with threats of a lawsuit and her answer to confrontations with her daughter is physical violence.

Correctional professionals who resort to a confrontational approach on a regular basis likely see themselves as persons responsible for punishing inmates. With a competing conflict-management style, the inmates know just where they stand, in other words, against the system. There is a no-win situation. The staff loses because working conditions and attitudes are negative and inmates lose because they are subject to constant intimidation.

There is a time and a place when confrontation is necessary. It should be used sparingly. Obviously, in self-defense situations, it is you against the offender. Training in self-defense equips the correctional professional to use only as much force as necessary and then to revert back to the cooperative style. The correctional professional is managing the conflict situation at all times, and control over one's behavior is always necessary.

When working with others, the correctional professional also is responsible for managing the response of coworkers. Using the cooperative and collaborative approach to restrain a coworker who is losing control in a confrontational situation may be necessary. In a confrontation with the jail's correctional officer, Gail Overland, Cindy Hughes threw a container of urine on Gail. It was the responsibility of the other deputy to restrain Gail from entering the cell to teach Cindy a lesson by beating her up.

Whether it is Rodney King on parole, a belligerent inmate, or an illegal migrant worker, when a person does not cooperate, it is not open season for violence. It is the responsibility of the coworker to manage every conflict situation. It is understandable when working with people in trouble with the law to become frustrated and develop a negative attitude. One is reminded of the study conducted at Stanford University over twenty years ago that had to be stopped after only two days when college students playing the role of correctional officers became too negative and confrontational with students playing the role of inmates. That was only two days. Think what this type of environment can do to a career correctional professional.

In thirty years of policing, the author's father prided himself in only having to shoot his gun once, and that was when it was proper to do so as a warning shot. The person who was fleeing stopped. The writer's brother said he was kicked once by a perpetrator as he was placing him in the police car, and, by instinct, he kicked back. It bothers him to this day that he did not manage that situation as a professional. In thirty-five years in corrections, although this writer boxed in the ring and had thirty-one amateur fights, he never hit an inmate in an institution or a person under his supervision in the community. However, he did warn parties that if they did not cooperate, other actions could be taken.

Self-defense can justify managed physical confrontation. This correctional professional preferred to talk to each individual person-to-person, and when he asked for their cooperation, he received it. Most people respond according to the way they are dealt with by the other party.

Sometimes confrontation is necessary, as when a correctional officer is being attacked physically. But this physical confrontation also can be managed. By stepping in with assistance, the assault can be stopped with the threat of a physical response to restrain the offending party. Often, the threat of confrontation is all that is necessary. If self-defense techniques learned in training become necessary, then they should be used with restraint.

Once the correctional professionals have stopped the resistance and have regained control, they should attempt to obtain the offenders' cooperation. If the correctional professionals speak calmly, often the offenders will respond with cooperation. After the physical confrontation, the inmate will respect the correctional officer if the proper restraints were used. If the professional shouts at the offender, often the offender will shout back, and the matter can escalate. Or, the inmate will shut up but hold a grudge, spread the word, and look for ways to seek payback.

A poor use of confrontation is simply to wade in with a club and ask questions later. It makes a bad situation worse. Only as much force as is needed should be employed. The tendency to retaliate by teaching the inmate a lesson only serves to reinforce the inmate's negative attitude and belief that might does make right. Fear and intimidation are not the tools that a constructive correctional professional uses to build a good working and living environment. A crisis management situation requires more use of the head than the hand.

Swearing is a form of verbal violence and is confrontation, word for word. It is all too common in a correctional environment. Staff, inmates, probationers, and parolees use it like a comma. Swearing reinforces violence, as in the "F" word, which denigrates women and literally connotes rape. The "MF" term literally refers to incest. The "B" word, in particular, puts women down, refers to them as female dogs, and reinforces disrespect.

Can a professional correctional officer control his or her language and thereby serve as a role model to coworkers and offenders? Or, does the correctional professional join the ranks of the many and perpetuate the atmosphere of their community with terms of degradation? This may be an impossible task, but that does not mean it should not be addressed. Youth leaders in the community now are encouraging young people to look at their street language and see it as a real means of either showing respect or reinforcing negative feelings. It often is the first step to violence. As correctional professionals, serving as role models and conflict managers, using the right vocabulary can be more important than it appears. All correctional professionals have to make that decision for themselves. Think about it.

Domestic violence is directly related to a confrontational and controlling style. Violence spills over on the job and at home. Domestic violence is a crime—often assault—and there is no excuse for it. No one deserves to be hit unless in self-defense, and a professional conflict manager in the corrections field has to have control at all times. Correctional and law enforcement personnel have a particular problem with domestic violence and sexual harassment. It often is aggravated by alcohol and stress. If a correctional officer routinely uses a confrontational style to manage conflict, it can have devastating effects personally and professionally on everyone.

Probation officer Bill Sinclair must address the domestic violence in probationer Nate Carter's relationship with Tina Lopez. Sinclair should refer Nate to a program for batterers as a condition of probation. His girlfriend should receive counseling from a program that serves domestic violence victims.

Cindy Hughes also should attend anger management to deal with her relationships with her boyfriend and her daughter. Her probation officer, Joyce Hennessey, has a real opportunity to effect Cindy's future behavior. She then can reinforce what Cindy has learned each time an incident arises that was handled well or could have been managed better. Cindy can learn that she herself can and should be managing her own life.

A Conflict Management Test
For the Correctional Professional

How are you as a correctional conflict manager? Read the following scenarios and give your usual response. Do not try to figure out what the right answer should be. Only you have the right answer for you. Answer what you normally do or would do in the given situation. Remember, you are trying to evaluate your conflict-management style and determine whether you should look at your approach and perhaps work on it to be a more effective correctional professional. This test may be a good indicator for you.

Following question #15 is a table for you to write in your answers. If you frequently would respond to the given situation in a certain way, write "3" after the question number. If you occasionally would respond this way, write a "2." If you would rarely respond this way, write a "1."

1. If a correctional client gives me a hard time, I threaten him with a negative report in his file or a violation, or I will stand nose-to-nose to show him who is in charge.

2. If a correctional client starts explaining her point of view regarding a conflict, I usually listen and explain my own position.

3. I look for middle ground in any coworker dispute.

4. If a problem arises, I admit that I may be wrong and can see the other person's point of view, but as a correctional professional, I have a job to do.

5. If a correctional client raises an issue, I just stare at him and ignore him until he leaves, or I tell him to move on.

6. In any conflict, I firmly pursue my goals and objectives.

7. When there is a disagreement, I attempt to diffuse the conflict by looking for issues on which we both agree.

8. In any dispute, I try to reach some sort of position with which we can both live.

9. With other staff, I usually give in when a conflict arises to keep the problem from escalating and getting out of hand.

10. If someone brings up a complaint, I try to change the subject and go about my work.

11. In any dispute, I argue until I get my way.

12. In conflict situations, I try to get everything out in the open.

13. If I have a problem with anyone, I try to give a little and get the other person to give a little also.

14. If someone presents a problem, I pretend to understand and agree and then just do my job.

15. When a disagreement pops up, I try to lighten up the situation with a joke.

I	II	III	IV	V
1 _____	2 _____	3 _____	4 _____	5 _____
6 _____	7 _____	8 _____	9 _____	10 _____
11 _____	12 _____	13 _____	14 _____	15 _____
Totals: _____	_____	_____	_____	_____

Analysis: Add up the numbers in each column. Review your highest score. Do you feel this reflects your conflict-management style? Review your other scores.

Column one: If the score is high in this area, it indicates a confrontative and competing style, a hard bargainer with a might-makes-right attitude. Personal concerns are being pursued at the other individual's expense, and the goal is to win.

Column Two: This is the cooperative, collaborative approach. Working together is important. Negotiating and exploring disagreements, generating alternatives, and finding a solution that satisfies both parties is the goal. There is a win-win motivation.

Column Three: This is the compromising position. Both parties win to a certain degree.

Column Four: This is the soft bargainer who believes in killing the other party with kindness. The other person's point of view prevails at the time of the conflict, but a later victory over the party when the stakes are bigger is likely the goal. The soft bargainer lets the other side win for the time being.

Column Five: This person relies on avoidance. It is the most used conflict-management style and leaves the conflict unaddressed. The hope is that by doing nothing, the problem will go away—or at least it will be postponed for a while—and maybe someone else will solve the problem. Both sides often lose.

All five conflict management approaches can be used effectively depending on the person and the situation. If the highest score is in column one—the confrontative and competing area—you should evaluate your long-term goals. The immediate conflict may be discouraged, but the resentment may be right under the surface. The inmate, probationer, or parolee also is learning that might really does mean right and authority rules. They then use the learned strategy on their peers and family. The potential for an abuse of power exists. Restoring what is right and fair is not even considered. It is a "my way or the highway" approach.

If column two is the highest score, the focus is on cooperation and collaboration. Consistently, this will be the most effective approach in the long run. Communication is possible and information is shared. Both parties win. This is the preferred conflict-management style for the correctional professional.

A high score in column three indicates a compromising mode that can be effective at times, but as a general principle, it has its limitations.

The fourth column reveals an accommodating conflict style, and the person who relies on this style runs the greatest risk of being manipulated, which every correctional professional fears. It also can end in burnout or an attitude that nothing really makes a difference anyway. This type of worker is not very effective.

A high score in column five is also a danger. Avoidance is traditionally the most used style. It signals that the person is not taking responsibility for conflict in his or her life and prefers to get by rather than become involved. It also is a sign of burnout and a defeatist attitude. Interpersonal skills are at a minimum.

Where do you stand based on the results of this test? Again, take this as an indication of your conflict-management style and learn from it.

Chapter III

Cooperation and Collaboration, the Key Ingredients in Corrections

There are no quick fixes in the field of corrections, but there are some everyday approaches that can make life a lot more tolerable and can be effective at the same time. In corrections, whether in the community or in the institution, interaction with staff and clients is the key area that must be addressed regularly. If one has an attitude that this is just a job, then the adversarial approach will win out because you view the other person as the problem.

In conflict management, a win-win outcome is desirable. If both the staff and the offender feel the interaction was fair, the work environment and the personal fulfillment can be satisfying. For example, when Nate Carter and his employer sit down and agree on the problems at work and how to address them, they both win. Nate keeps his job and the employer does not have to hire and train someone else. Cindy Hughes and her daughter, Lily, working with a parent-child mediator, communicate their feelings and frustration and work out a better mother-daughter relationship.

If a staff or offender loses, then there will be hostility and it will be payback time in the near future. A staff person who is always late is reported by another staff person. The one reporting puts pressure on her peer and feels this may solve the problem and make her job easier. The reported staff member has a bad record in the file and holds it against the other staff person. If staff and offender both lose in a confrontation, the entire community suffers. This might involve an out-of-control verbal exchange or even a physical fight between a correctional officer and an inmate. Both could suffer injury and put the entire institutional community on edge.

How Can You Obtain a Win-win Outcome?

Cooperation and collaboration are the key components for an effective conflict manager. All of the other conflict-management approaches are useful at the right time and at the right place, but the cooperative and collaborative technique is the most satisfying and effective one. Two heads are better than one. Negotiating and working together by exploring a disagreement and looking at alternatives allows both parties to have ownership of a mutually agreeable solution.

The conflict manager who uses cooperation and collaboration in life can have a more harmonious experience in family interactions, in friendships, in neighborhood contacts, and in the workplace. Who says one has to leave effective human dynamics such as conflict-management techniques at the door of the detention facility, correctional facility, or probation or parole office? Conflict resolution skills not only are needed in the correctional milieu, they are essential if we are to make a difference.

For a variety of reasons, correctional professionals may find the cooperative and collaborative approach in conflict management to be counterintuitive and, in some cases, even dangerous. Common concerns involve the loss of power and authority, fear of manipulation, lack of time, and the need for respect.

Power, Control, and Authority

There is a real concern among correctional professionals that if they use a cooperative and collaborative conflict-management style, they will lose their authority and control over their clients. In turn, they fear that as professionals, they will not have the power to manage anything. They will appear weak. Consequently, the correctional community continues to use methods that will keep these fears from being realized. The community confronts any effort to introduce a different approach to working with the difficult population that enters the criminal justice system. Using avoidance, confrontation, and a punishment modality, the system goes on and real opportunity for change is lost.

There is no need to fear appearing weak or lacking power, control, or authority if all the conflict-management and conflict-resolution tools are used appropriately. In fact, a confident conflict manager in corrections will be respected and seen as fair and strong.

Manipulation

Manipulation is a major fear of people in the criminal justice business. It is a reality that must be faced in every human interaction; it does not have to be feared. Confident, well-trained correctional officers, probation and parole agents, and staff people in community-based corrections programs have two eyes and two ears and can read efforts by staff, the public, and the client when manipulation surfaces. In a dialog or exchange, this type of effort can be identified immediately and dealt with for what it is.

People learn their behavior, and if the correctional professional can teach the client better ways to solve problems, then manipulation will go back to its normal use and not be the obstacle it presently is in corrections. For example, Cindy Hughes tries to manipulate the system by claiming racism whenever it is convenient. Knowing that there is racism in society, using this tactic is a safe bet to make staff back off and lighten up on her. Staff are then more concerned about the manipulation than about working constructively with Cindy. The correctional professional can do nothing (avoidance), and Cindy gets away with it again, or the correctional professional could confront Cindy with her manipulation and tell her that she cannot pull that all the time. She then will try to escalate the issue or internalize it and feel justified. The conflict manager will respect her point of view and tell her that she is entitled to her opinion but would like her to cooperate so they both can do what is necessary to address the present problem.

Time

Correctional professionals may believe that they do not have time to listen and learn the nature of each conflict situation with inmates, probationers, or parolees. Efficient correctional professionals can elicit cooperation from the client without taking an inordinate amount of time from their work responsibilities. It is an opportunity to teach the person how to deal with people and conflicts. The inmate has nothing but time. The probationer and parolee must meet the conditions of their supervision. Perhaps correctional professionals should take only as much time as is practical and available, but they should not lose sight of the overall goal, which is to help the client change negative behavior into positive behavior.

For example, if the correctional officer is processing a series of inmates on a work detail and one inmate begins to ask a number of questions, the correctional officer can ignore the inmate or quickly tell him that he does not have time (avoidance) or gruffly tell him to shut up and keep moving (confrontation) or, as a conflict manager, quickly tell him the answer, if possible, or tell him, "I don't have time to answer you now, but I'll get back to you in a minute." The correctional professional is managing a time conflict and also is asking for the inmate's cooperation. The most important thing is that the correctional officer is taking the limited amount of time to teach the inmate again.

Respect

Everyone wants to be respected as a human being. Many young people who have committed violent crimes say they were "dissed" by their victims. They were shown disrespect and put down in front of their peers, and they acted out to retaliate. In an interview shortly before his death, Dr. Benjamin Spock was asked why young people were more violent today. What once was a fistfight now becomes a drive-by shooting. He stated that he believed it all stemmed from a lack of respect shown to young people who learn this approach; then, the young person, in turn, has no respect for any other person or even life itself.

Offenders cannot be respected for what they have done, but they never should lose the correctional professional's respect for their basic humanity. We condemn the concentration camps during World War II. We do not want to be accused of that type of mentality.

Inmates are still human beings. They do not have to earn our respect for that. Whether the person is a prisoner of war, a child molester, a terrorist, a convicted minister, or a former chief judge, his or her dignity as a human being always should be respected.

In corrections, staff frequently unofficially classify clients into two categories: "a—holes" or "okay." To ask for cooperation and collaboration from the okay offenders is reasonable, but is it realistic even to try that approach with the other kind? The answer is, "yes." Will the ideal conflict-management approach work with the difficult client? Not all the time and probably not at all at first. There are certain inmates who are not ready to change. That is the challenge for the correctional professional. Do not give up your standards because clients have an attitude or are possibly mentally unstable. That is their problem. Do not make it your problem. Even people who are serving life sentences or who committed cold, heinous crimes can be reached if they are given consistent, fair treatment in a correctional institution. That is why there is the need for a variety of tools to work successfully in a corrections environment.

When the professional correctional staff person tries to serve as a role model to the client, all the conflict-management approaches must be employed. If the client does not respond to the request to cooperate and work together, then the correctional professional can explain what the consequences are, and the next time the opportunity arises they have another chance to respond cooperatively. Some people never will change for their own reasons. The majority, however, will learn, if shown, the proper respect and if given the chance, they will try new behaviors. In this process, a cooperative and collaborative community is created. This type of environment helps all concerned.

TALK

A handy formula and practical guide for personal interaction and conflict management is called the "TALK" approach, which stands for Teach each other And Listen to share information and Knowledge. This can be a common-sense tool for the practitioner. How does it work?

In the TALK formula, the answer to conflict management is to encourage cooperation and collaboration. Cooperation and collaboration both require that the parties work together (operate together and labor together). If both sides listen to what the other side is saying and learn from each other, then information is shared. With the correct information, decisions can be made and the problem—not the person—can be attacked, and a resolution often can be achieved.

For example, an inmate's phone time is up, and she will not hang up to give the next person her turn. The correctional officer can do nothing—avoidance—which leaves the other inmates upset or they expect the same privilege. Or, the correctional officer can confront the offender by giving her the evil eye or the thumb's-out sign or verbally tell her to get off. The officer even can come up and take the phone out of the person's hand. The inmate likely will feel that she was not shown any respect and that she was put down in front of her peers; likely, she will look for opportunities to retaliate either against the staff or against other inmates to regain her status in the population. If the inmate also has a low self-esteem level, this experience reinforces those feelings. This type of action unnecessarily can cause unrest in the institution and slowly boil over into a real confrontation.

The cooperative and collaborative approach would be to come up to the person and tell her that her time is up. One person, the correctional professional, is doing her job, and the other person, the inmate, is responding. One human being talks to another human being. The inmate then can cooperate or provide an explanation that the correctional professional could not anticipate, such as that her child is sick and she is speaking with her child's doctor.

Is she manipulating the situation? If she is, the officer can see a pattern and talk to her about her behavior. If the correctional professional does nothing, the officer loses, and the other inmates lose because the inmate on the phone will think that she has taken advantage of the system. Avoidance only will encourage the inmate to try the same behavior again.

In confronting the inmate, the officer will win temporarily, and the inmate will lose, unless the confrontation escalates, in which case both the officer and the inmate can lose. The other inmates learn that might makes right. By taking the time to listen for the reason for the delay, the officer shows respect to an appreciative inmate. Done in a professional and humane manner, it teaches the other inmates to listen and learn before they act or jump to conclusions. Too simple? Remember, the formula is to keep it simple and not to complicate every interaction.

Another example involves a teacher in a correctional facility or a community-based program working with a class. One student in the back appears to be sleeping. The instructor can ignore it and simply say that is his problem and when he is ready to learn, he will pay attention. The opposite approach is to yell at the sleeping student and tell him that if he does not pay attention, he can be kicked out and sent back to the cellblock or be written up as noncooperative and be in jeopardy of being revoked from the community program.

The conflict manager could take this challenge as an opportunity to teach the entire class about conflict management and cooperation. The teacher may say to the class, "We have one of our people trying to sleep in the back of the classroom. Should we let him sleep and do nothing (avoidance) or should we threaten him with expulsion (confrontation)? How about if we TALK to him and find out what the problem is and ask for his cooperation?" The tendency is to miss opportunities like these and do what is easier.

One concern is that the correctional staff cannot babysit or pay attention to each inmate's personal whims. The answer to that legitimate concern is that by listening and learning, the correctional professionals really are doing their job. They are teaching inmates how to communicate and cooperate in a problem situation. Inmates will see this effort and future interactions with them can be more productive. It also will be more productive for the correctional officer in the long run to be informed and act wisely than to move everything along and have to pay for it later through a negative attitude and a hostile environment.

Probation or parole officers often are seen as counselors for their clients, but correctional officers do not see their role as "counselors." This author is not calling the correctional officer a "counselor" either. The correctional officer is, however, a conflict manager. Normal human interactions are not "counseling." Whether it is talking to your child, spouse, neighbor, co-worker or an inmate, the correctional officer must use conflict-management tools to deal with situations and to build better relationships.

Although both avoidance and confrontative approaches to conflict can be effective and sometimes are necessary in given conflict situations, they are usually the worst ways to deal with problems and people because they are adversarial, and both sides either lose or one side wins for the time being and the other side waits for retaliation or harbors resentment. Avoidance and confrontation are called "flight or fight." If avoidance or confrontation is needed, the conflict manager quickly should return to a spirit of cooperation and collaboration as soon as possible. The persons being avoided or confronted see that if they do not cooperate, other consequences will result. They learn that cooperation on both sides is in their own best interest and in the staff persons'.

Here is another example. A correctional officer approaches a cell that an inmate refuses to leave. The officer can lock the inmate down in the cell and leave him for someone else to deal with; the officer likely will be criticized by his superior for not taking any action. The inmate wins temporarily, and the officer loses and is viewed by the other inmates as weak. If the correctional officer adopts a confrontative approach, he can threaten or even jerk up the inmate, or the officer can call for backup and "teach the inmate a lesson." In this scenario, the correctional officer wins and the inmate loses. The inmates again conclude that might makes right, and they will continue to use the same methods in their dealings with other inmates, associates, and staff.

In the cooperative mode, the officer asks the inmate why he is not moving. Through dialog, the officer can obtain answers. With the correct information, the officer can make an informed decision. If the inmate cooperates because the officer listened to him, everyone wins. If there is no cooperation on the part of the inmate, the officer can explain the consequences and, if necessary, call for back-up to physically remove the inmate from his cell. A competent person never has to resort to violence. Firm physical effort does not need to be violent. A parent can physically pick up a disruptive child without being violent. A correctional officer can use his training to physically move an inmate without resorting to violence. In an extreme situation, self-defense may call for stronger action, especially if the inmate is armed with a homemade weapon.

Another scenario in which a correctional professional can use the TALK approach is when she comes into the common TV room during an argument over programming between two inmates. The officer can avoid the situation and just walk out, and allow the inmates to work out their own problems. If a serious fight breaks out, the correctional professional missed the opportunity to prevent it. If the staff person instead confronts the inmates by turning off the television and announcing that the inmates have lost their viewing privileges, then she wins for the time being and all the inmates involved lose.

The better approach is for the correctional officer to see this as an opportunity to practice crisis management using the TALK method. By stepping in and using the mediation model on a small scale, she can tell the conflicting parties that she will facilitate their dispute and ask both parties to talk about their respective positions. The television can be turned off while the parties negotiate their dispute. Experience has shown that if this occurs, all parties quiet down and seriously begin to express themselves. They learn that talking out a problem is better than acting out their frustrations.

Usually, the parties will reach their own solution. If the parties cannot reach an acceptable solution, the correctional officer can arbitrate the matter based on the information shared, and she can hand down a decision. The inmates will appreciate that the correctional professional gave them an opportunity to resolve the problem on their own terms, and they will accept the arbitration decision as the next logical step after their inability to develop their own solution. The next time a crisis arises, the same group of inmates will be ready to talk out the problem rather than fight it out.

One further example of the TALK approach with staff is the case of a fellow worker coming late on a regular basis. The person he or she is relieving can do nothing and puts up with the behavior, thereby losing while the other person is getting away with it. Or, the individual can confront his replacement and threaten to report him to their supervisor. Now, the late person is angry and makes life miserable for everybody. This is a lose-lose situation. The cooperative conflict manager talks to the person one-on-one without others listening and learns the reason for the tardiness. The parties can agree that if it continues, other action will be taken. Both people can win with communication and cooperation. TALK it out. As human beings, we have the capability to talk to each other. With the rise of violence in society, more talking is needed. As professionals in corrections, let's TALK THE TALK and WALK THE WALK.

Is the cooperative and collaborative approach a sign of weakness? Will cooperative correctional professionals be accused of collaborating with the enemy? Will every client or coworker try to manipulate the cooperative conflict manager? The answer to these very good questions is, "No!" Well-trained correctional professionals have self-assurance and the ability to communicate with other staff and clients; they can establish an effective conflict-management style that will come across to everyone they encounter. Wisely deciding when to use the right conflict-management approach is the key to managing conflict effectively. To be confident, put the cooperative and collaborative formula in your toolchest and use it as your major strategy. It can make life more interesting, challenging, and rewarding. Best of all, it can make you more effective and create a better working relationship with everyone in your correctional community. Ultimately, it can make work actually easier and more enjoyable. It also spills over to your home life and community. The correctional professional cannot change the world but can help change one person at a time for the better.

Chapter IV

The Correctional Staff and Conflict

All correctional staff need to be trained in effective conflict-management and conflict-resolution skills. Yes, this includes self-defense and security measures, but the majority of the training should focus on preventing the need for physical intervention. With proper training, staff can create an atmosphere where people can live and work in relative harmony. Without an adversarial outlook dominating the landscape, both staff and client can put their energy towards positive measures rather than wasting their time perpetuating the "us versus them" mentality.

In the correctional facility, staff are role models to the inmate. As role models, they can become a positive force. Supervision is a major responsibility, but it can be incorporated into the bigger picture that relates to helping the inmate begin to function as a productive person. Staff do not have to feel that they are the real prisoners with golden handcuffs—salary and benefits—assigned to babysit a bunch of immature predators.

Many correctional facilities are in rural areas, but the majority of the inmates come from urban settings. Accordingly, the staff and the inmates frequently have different backgrounds. There can be racial and language differences, cultural distinctions, and a "street" separation. In an effort to bridge these gaps, more women and minorities are being hired. This can improve understanding and awareness and provide a better natural balance to the population. However, if a person has to move from the urban home area to accept a position or a promotion in a rural area, that individual may not be in the best mood to interact constructively with a belligerent, hostile inmate. Patience and tolerance may not be on the top of the attitude scale for either the inmate or the correctional staff. In those cases, the conflict-management skills come more into play than ever.

With the approach that the role of the correctional staff is to listen to the inmate, to learn where the inmate is coming from, and to communicate positive behavior patterns, the desired effect can be catching and often is realized. The working conditions can improve, the attitude of the staff and inmate can become more cooperative, and the inmate upon release can be prepared better to function in society. What the inmate learns from the staff is that listening and learning works better than walking away and ignoring the needs of the other person or barking demands and threatening dire consequences. Avoidance and confrontation temporarily may enhance a person's reputation, but is it worth spending years as a staff person or inmate playing games of bluff or facing nonverbal, verbal, or physical intimidation?

If the approach is to warehouse inmates and punish them at every turn and just put in the time for the paycheck, the benefits, and future retirement, then it is business as usual. The conditions will continue to be uncomfortable, and the recidivism rates will continue to be high. Society will be in more danger because the inmate who arrived at the facility angry at the world now comes out more hostile after having learned from society's keepers that power and control are the name of the game.

If inmates experience a sense of positive community in the correctional institution, they can help create a positive community on the outside. With the support of that community, the likelihood of falling back into the same negative behaviors decreases. As an alcoholic benefits from an Alcoholics Anonymous group, so, too, does an inmate benefit from a supportive community environment.

Staff trained in conflict management and conflict resolution not only can work better with the inmate population in crisis management situations, but these skills can be used in day-to-day interaction with other staff and the public, and they can be brought back to the family so that the homefront does not have to suffer from the frustrations of the job. If staff members have a better feeling about their work, this carries over to the way they relate to their spouse, children, relatives, and neighbors. In the justice system, there are high rates of alcohol use and abuse, domestic violence, divorce, stress, and suicide. It is not very efficient to have a course on stress management if conflict-management and conflict-resolution training are not included. Conflict-management and conflict-resolution training is limited if it focuses only on control and not on the long-term goal of restoring a sense of justice to all by listening to and learning from the people involved.

There is a tendency in the corrections field to get tired of dealing with "screw ups" every day. The new correctional officer with the best intentions often learns from the veteran officers that the inmates are born losers and that the best approach is either to ignore them—avoidance—or to let them know who is boss—confrontation. Of course, the inmate expects this type of attitude and begins to fulfill this prophecy. The work environment continues in this cycle. For the correctional officers who are their own persons and who try to put the best conflict-management and conflict-resolution principles into practice, life and work can become more challenging, interesting, and rewarding. Burnout is usually more of an attitude problem than the result of growing tired of one's job.

Training

Conflict-management and conflict-resolution procedures should be a core part of every correctional person's initial training, and refresher courses should be repeated every three years. Pretests on conflict-management and resolution styles can be given; then, periodically people can be retested to determine changes in their conflict-management approaches. Staff can learn the basics on conflict management and then participate in a series of role plays based on situations commonly experienced in the correctional environment. This can include conflicts that offenders have with each other, authority, family, work situations, and conflicts among staff. In refresher courses, the staff can create situations that actually were handled and review what worked, why, and what could have been done differently.

One of the most important units in training is how the staff can translate conflict-management and conflict-resolution skills for the client. This is done through being a role model and in conducting actual classes in conflict management for the inmate, probationer, or parolee. Again, if the client learns these skills, it makes the job of the correctional professional easier, and it helps the client to function better in any situation. It empowers the staff and the inmate to experience success and to have positive control over the situation. Energy is exerted in managing the situation, negotiating, and in solving the problem rather than posturing for a reputation or temporary control.

When an incident happens in the institution, staff always should review and study the situation and learn from it. If the philosophy of the institution is to have all staff see their role as teachers of problem-solving skills, then a united effort can be effective. For example, if there is a fight in the corridor between two rival gangs and it is broken up and the inmates are separated and placed in special housing, the incident not only should be written up and the consequences handed out, but the matter should be seen as a conflict-management challenge. Instead of informally talking about what happened, the supervisors should have follow-up training on what went right and what went wrong based on conflict-management techniques. Questions should focus on why the altercation happened, what can be done to address the reasons for the incident, who can talk to the inmates individually or in their respective groups as to the future, and how problems can be handled. A mediation possibly could take place between the gang leaders and an institutional mediator and a trained inmate mediator.

Informants

In the criminal justice system, correctional professionals need to gather information to know what is happening and to prevent situations from occurring, continuing, and escalating. In conflict management and conflict resolution, knowledge is power. It can prevent something from happening or heal a rift that has been opened. Rather than viewing the exchange of information as "snitching" or seeing the informant as a "rat," staff and inmates alike should learn to see the informant as a person who is out to improve the correctional community.

Here is one example based on the author's experience with informants. (For another example of how conflict-management skills can lead to cooperation with authorities, see Chapter VII.) It occurred when the author ran a community-based alternative to incarceration program. A resident notified this writer in confidence that one of the other clients kept two guns in his room. A quick search confirmed the information and led to the expulsion of the person from the program and his return to prison. The informant saved the other clients and the community from any possible altercation and from additional crimes. We told the informant that he was not snitching but was helping his immediate community, his fellow program members, and the community at large by preventing any future violence.

In a house meeting that night, we talked to the group and told them it was their responsibility to help each other when circumstances like this develop. We did not reveal that someone came forward, but we did tell them that we all are in jeopardy when events like this happen. We also told them that conveying this information is an excellent way for them to repair the harm done by their past crimes and to help their fellow program members by preventing them from getting into future trouble.

Chapter V

The Correctional Client and Conflict

Inmates should be taught conflict-management and conflict-resolution skills while they are in the institution so that they can have a better living environment and correctional staff can have a safer, more fulfilling, and effective work experience. These skills provide the inmates with a daily opportunity to demonstrate their desire to repay society for the wrong they have done. It is not just at a parole hearing that they become model prisoners. They have an opportunity every day with staff and other inmates. Rather than just "doing time" one day after another, the inmates are serving society by trying to do what is right; they can begin to restore a sense of justice to everyone with whom they come into contact. These efforts must begin in the institution to become part of their lifestyle.

The second reason to teach inmates conflict-management skills is to prepare them to use these skills in their relationships now—with other inmates, staff, and family members—and with their family, peers, and in their work relationships when they return to society. If inmates are not willing to repair the harm done by their crimes while they are in the institution, then they will not change magically when they are released.

Many people are incarcerated because they did not handle conflict correctly in their daily interactions while they were in the community. They either avoided responsibilities through the use or abuse of drugs (alcohol, still number one) or they acted out their anger through violent acts (assault, rape, robbery, and so forth). In working with residents at a halfway house, the author asked if anyone there believed they were incarcerated for not managing conflict well. One resident responded quicker than the rest. He explained that he had trouble with his girlfriend's former boyfriend. While he was visiting his girlfriend one day, a brick was thrown through her apartment window. He immediately ran down and got in a fight with her former boyfriend. The boyfriend was seriously injured. The resident was convicted of assault, and based on his former record, he was incarcerated.

Now in a halfway house, we used the TALK approach to analyze with the group what he could have done. Avoidance meant doing nothing and losing face with his girlfriend. He tried confrontation and found out what the consequences were for that choice. How he could try to talk to this person was discussed. Having a third party, a friend of both of theirs who they trusted was another option. Calling the police was offered as a temporary solution. The residents pointed out that the problem still would be there. They concluded that he should have tried to talk to the person or have the friend serve as a mediator. One resident after the other gave similar examples and enjoyed talking out solutions, whereas in the past they either went off and got high or acted violently to confront the problem.

If half of what is called crime is between people who know each other (Bureau of Justice Statistics, Criminal Victimization in the United States, 1994) then, it may be prevented if the parties know how to manage and resolve problem situations. Recidivism can be reduced if inmates manage conflict in their lives.

Avoidance is the key to drug use and abuse. To escape situations, a person goes off and gets drunk on alcohol or high on narcotics. A three-year study by the National Center on Addiction and Substance Abuse at Columbia University (CASA) indicates that 80 percent of people in prison are seriously involved with drugs and alcohol. Flight or running away from responsibilities is a sign of immaturity, and it leads to criminal behavior. This could be defined as a medical problem. If people are treated for their dependency and required to address what caused them to turn to chemicals to feel better and medicate themselves, it could be a way to reduce crime.

If inmates learn conflict-management and conflict-resolution skills—particularly how to negotiate and mediate problems—while they are in prison, not only will they make more productive use of their time while they are in the institution, but they will carry these new found tools with them and use these skills with their families, friends, and neighbors for the rest of their lives. Inmates often are eager to learn; once they have grasped the basics of conflict management and conflict resolution, they can teach other inmates both formally and informally.

One staff person can supervise the training that over time can include the entire inmate population. For example, a staff member can receive conflict-management training from the local university or college and then conduct a class for interested staff and inmates. From that group, a core of people can conduct the training for other interested staff and inmates. If the warden believes it is worthwhile, it could become mandatory for all staff and available to interested inmates. If it is taught by a staff and inmate team, the interest may spread throughout the population. It would be interesting to observe the change in incidents once a program of this nature has been institutionalized. If and when problems arise, they can become opportunities to learn rather than only a danger to fear or another headache that goes with the territory.

Is this a practical solution, and can it really be done in a correctional facility? It is being done. One example is a program at the Washington State Reformatory, The Inside Mediation Program. Thirty inmates have been trained in mediation and are used to settle prison disputes. The program helps reduce tension because now people have to accept responsibility for their own actions and work out agreeable solutions. Participants learn new ways of thinking and of communicating. It gives them a sense of respect and a sense of value. For information write: Laura Pierson, Program Manager, The Inside Mediation Program, P.O. Box 839, Everett, Washington 98206.

Chapter VI

Probation, Parole, Day, and Residential Programs

Most of the answers to offenders' behavioral problems are in our communities, and these resources should be available to the person who is not dangerous and is able to benefit from opportunities to obtain gainful employment, counseling, and educational advancement. A program on how to manage conflict and resolve problems for probationers and parolees would pay great dividends. Since the person is already under community supervision, a requirement to attend seminars on conflict management makes sense. How could it work?

Probation

As individuals are assigned to probation, an assessment can be made regarding how they have dealt with conflict in the past. If persons have used avoidance or confrontation as the primary answer to handling problems, that individual should be required to attend the seminar sessions on conflict management and conflict resolution as a condition of probation. Saturday or evening classes should be available depending on the work schedules of the participants. The course could be taught by an experienced probation officer trained in conflict management and conflict resolution, or it could be offered by a trained volunteer from the local business community or an educational institution who can make the course relevant to the probationer.

A series of sessions could be held on the basics of conflict management, negotiations, and conflict resolution, and the lessons from those seminars could be applied to the participants' personal lives. Areas to be covered would include individual conflict-management styles, negotiation and conflict resolution strategies, personal relationships, the work environment, living arrangements (for example, landlord-tenant relationships), neighborhood interactions, peer groups, and the criminal justice system—in other words, police, probation officer, sheriff's deputies, jailers, and judges. During each session, probationers would bring up real conflicts they have experienced and role play the way it happened and what could or should have been done.

After the completion of the course, any conflict situations can serve as opportunities to discuss how the conflict-management and conflict-resolution techniques are being applied. When the old ways of dealing with conflict surface, the probation officer can role play with the probationer and determine what went wrong and why. New behaviors can be learned. For example, Nate Carter and Cindy Hughes could have worked with their respective probation officers regarding conflicts on work, family, and living arrangements. Putting the responsibility on the probationers to solve their own problems and giving them the basic skills to accomplish it will go a long way toward helping others help themselves.

The meeting with the probation officer can be a productive interaction rather than a simple check in or a general "how is everything going" routine. If the participants are successful, they can influence those around them, and the entire atmosphere can be changed at work, school, and home. In our case studies, Nate Carter and Cindy Hughes would have benefitted greatly from a course of this nature.

Parole

When individuals come out of a correctional facility, it takes a period of time for them to shake off the prison dust and adjust to not being institutionalized. Inside, it often is "three hots and a cot" and survival of the unfittest. Therefore, a number of behaviors must be unlearned. The parole agent again must assess the needs of the client and go through some of the same analysis as was described with the person on probation.

Added to the problem of institutionalization is the stigma of being an ex-convict. Employment is more difficult and family and friends are ready for the individual to fail. Conflict situations escalate, and patience and tolerance are reduced. If the person learned to react in a confrontational and competing style while growing up on the streets, and it was reinforced in the institution to survive, that same behavior too often is carried out into the community again. This makes the need for training in this area all the more important for the parolee.

For example, a parolee who experiences conflict on the job can do nothing—avoidance—and adopt a defeatist attitude and quit. Or, he can tell the boss what she can do with her job—confrontation—and use that as an excuse for dragging his feet on finding something else. Or, he can use a cooperative "let's work together" approach to find out what his boss' concerns are, express his own perception of the job situation, and work with his boss to obtain a win-win situation. If this occurs, the job gets done better, and the employee feels he was shown respect and heard. The parole officer can use mediation when a problem arises at the parolee's home or job. She can tell the parties that she is there to help both people resolve the problem (see Chapter VII).

It often is said that it may be too late for some people who have been through the criminal justice system time and time again to change. However, given better tools to manage conflict, the parolees can start anew and use the skills to address problems that in the past sank them.

Day and Residential Programs

In a day or evening program, the opportunity to follow up on conflict-management and conflict-resolution training is available on a regular basis. The chance for a change in conflict-management style is even greater. The individual client's reactions can be observed and reinforced every day in a positive manner. Both in a group setting and on an individual level, the person can see his behavior and its consequences, and he can talk about what changes can be made. In the past, this person would say the heck with it and go on with no hope for the future. In a day program, what is learned today can be practiced that day and reviewed the next day for success and reinforcement.

In a residential program—for example, a drug treatment center or halfway house—where the person lives and cannot get away with putting on an act, the true behaviors eventually come out. Conflict-management training can be taught and conflict situations can be experienced daily. It is like a family who really gets to know a brother or sister because they cannot be fooled by a false front. One expresses her true self in this type of setting. In this program, the person's natural family or significant other often can be part of the intervention and discussion. People must learn from their past and look to their future. See Chapter VIII for further information on probation, parole, and day and residential programs involving restorative justice.

The Conflict Management Sessions:
How Can These Ideas Be Implemented?

The opening session in a conflict-management class can be a frank discussion of the causes of conflict. The facilitator can explain that people have different perceptions and experiences and that conflict is okay. It is how a person handles the conflict that is important. Using the TALK (Teach

each other And Listen to each other to share information and Knowledge) method from Chapter III in the second class keeps the approach practical and gives the clients the idea that this is not complicated and that it can be part of their lifestyle.

If the clients are ready to go into more depth, use the methods discussed in Chapter II in the follow-up period. The trainer could use the next sessions to cover the key areas of the clients' lives and practice through role plays how to manage conflicts effectively. One session would cover what style the individuals normally use to work out conflict in their lives. The test in Chapter II can be adapted to the clients' needs, and they can see the consequences for their choices of conflict-management techniques.

Again, avoidance and confrontation are the most common management techniques, so be prepared to see these approaches used often. Another class period would address the interpersonal relationships with family members, including children and spouses or significant others. Children are a very important component because people learn their behavior, and if the children can learn right away that violence is not the answer, another generation may be saved from becoming victims or victimizers. Cindy Hughes can learn parenting skills and, in turn, her daughter, Lily, can learn that slapping and screaming at a child (confrontation) is not a productive way to deal with conflict.

Another important area to cover is conflict on the job. Ex-offenders often do not have as much trouble finding a job as they do keeping it. Part of the problem may be supervisors who have little tolerance for ex-offenders and who do not use good management techniques themselves. For example, an employer might not find out why the person missed work and then wonder why the individual has to be fired several weeks—and absences—later. People do not TALK to each other. Role playing with the clients prevents a series of failures by working through conflict situations so that the clients are not allowed to just walk off the job, but instead they have to talk about their feelings and look at their options before they can take any action.

It is easier to fail than to succeed, and one can sit back and blame others. If clients are trained to see conflict and manage it or resolve it through negotiation or mediation, then they can be successful in other phases of their lives.

In neighborhood interactions, conflicts with landlords, merchants, and other residents are part of everyday living. Positive interaction within the community not only can help individual and personal relationships, but it also can create harmony in the neighborhood. In every neighborhood there are key actors and leaders. With cooperation and collaboration, the benefits of working together can become contagious and affect the entire environment.

Training community volunteers to be mediators is taking place in every state. These community mediators help create harmony in their environment. If inmates, probationers, and parolees can be trained in conflict-management skills and learn mediation, then they can contribute constructively to their communities rather that being viewed as trouble makers and stereotyped as ex-cons. If they turn to mediation when a conflict that they cannot solve themselves arises, then incidents can be constructively addressed.

In New York City there was a major problem between the black community and a group of Korean grocery store owners. There was concern that every time a young black person came into one of these Korean-owned stores, the grocer thought the reason was to shoplift. The results were street protests and vandalism. A representative of the local community dispute resolution center sat down with representatives from both sides, and with funding from private businesses, proceeded to train black and Korean citizens as conflict managers and mediators. Whenever an incident arose in the future, it was referred for mediation for resolution rather than escalating to violence.

Peer groups can be the most difficult to crack. Peers remember the way it was. The reputation continues. If gang activity existed on the street or in the institution, it may be picked up again. This was this person's community. A new constructive community has to be developed. It is essential to spend at least a class working in this area. To go from a negative influence to a positive role model is a major hurdle. With group support and a new set of peers, it can be done. See also *Gangbusters* by Lonnie Jackson (American Correctional Association, 1998) for some suggestions on this.

The last session can be on the criminal justice system itself. People in trouble with the law have to realize that they are where they are because they did not handle conflict well. The logic is that if they try a different approach, they may have a different outcome. The way they interact with the police does determine how the police deal with them. How they cooperate with their probation officer or parole agent does make a difference. Nate Carter and Cindy Hughes do not have to be recidivists if they learn how to handle conflict constructively. Teaching offenders conflict-management and conflict-resolution skills will have an effect on the entire justice system. It does not have to be adversarial—us against them.

Chapter VII

Mediation, Victim and Offender Mediation, and Conflict Management and Resolution in Corrections

The conflict-management skills that have been discussed so far apply to general problem-solving and crisis situations. This chapter will concentrate on the use of mediation in corrections and how it can play an effective role in managing and resolving conflict.

Mediation

Mediation is a procedure in which two or more parties in a dispute voluntarily meet with a trained, neutral third person who assists in the resolution of the dispute. The parties decide together whether they can reach a mutually agreeable solution. This is different from a conciliation, in which the parties reach agreement by phone, letter, or third-party intervention—but without formally coming together in a mediation. It is also different from an arbitration, in which a third person makes a decision for the parties after listening to their evidence. Small claims court is an example of arbitration. Baseball salary disputes go before an arbitrator. Many businesses will have an arbitration clause in their contracts so the matter will be heard by an arbitrator rather than go to court. Mediation may be a better way to resolve many of these disputes.

Mediation can be a very helpful process for the field of corrections. It can range from staff-staff conflicts to staff-inmate difficulties, and from inmate-inmate disagreements to actual hostage situations and major facility disturbances. Probation officers and parole agents can use it for people under their supervision in a number of ways, including family matters, significant other relationships, employee-employer disagreements, and landlord-tenant squabbles. The probation officer or parole agent does not take sides but helps both parties work out agreeable solutions. In the process of mediation, the participants not only have a forum from which to communicate and talk to each other, but they have an opportunity to listen and learn what the problems are and what each person thinks can be a possible solution. This process also can involve family members during the incarceration stay and the inmate with prerelease plans in a correctional institution.

There is also a special type of mediation called victim and offender mediation where a victim of a crime requests to meet with the offender who committed the crime to obtain answers to questions the victim might have and to acquire more peace of mind and closure. It allows the offenders to be accountable for their actions, gives them a chance to see the consequences of their acts, and allows them to express any remorse to the persons they have victimized. It is a process that can be employed effectively when there is a need for restitution. The monetary amount can be agreed to by both parties and a realistic payment schedule can be determined. If there is an element of community service, the type and number of hours can be worked out together by the victim and the offender. This process also helps repair the community through community restitution and restores a sense of harmony. As a result, all the parties feel that a fair process was used to arrive at a mutual solution.

Training

The important ingredient for effective mediation is sufficient training. Proper training is between twenty-five and forty hours, including learning the theory, role playing, and observing. Institutional and community corrections staff can be trained and then can become a core of trainers after they gain experience mediating. Skilled probationers, parolees, and inmates can become part of the training team, as described in an earlier chapter. Initial training can be received through local universities, colleges, community dispute resolution centers, the American Arbitration Association, the Better Business Bureau in each location, and a number of private trainers.

Some of the most delinquent students in elementary and high schools make excellent mediators. The negative leaders now have a method to exert their strengths in a positive way. This can work in institutional and community corrections. Co-mediators can be used when the conflict is between staff and an inmate. One mediator can be a staff person and the other mediator can be an inmate. To have trained inmate mediators out in the population can be a real asset for any institution. The trust level for the inmate in the dispute will be there, and the word will go out that the administration is about addressing issues and not just controlling the population. All inmates who are trained will be valuable peacemakers in their institutions and when they leave, will carry those skills to any community they enter.

Examples of situations where mediation can be effective can range from gang-related incidents to correctional officer and inmate disagreements. This author once mediated a dispute between an inmate and his counselor. The inmate would not cooperate with a group-treatment program. He had made no progress and months of inactivity took place. In the mediation, the inmate stated what he felt the problem was and agreed to begin counseling again with a new individual counselor.

Another, more dramatic mediation took place between a state commissioner of corrections and the family of a young inmate who had run away from an open corrections camp and was killed in a robbery attempt. The mediation was an opportunity for the parents to obtain answers and for the commissioner to explain the limitations of the correctional system. How many commissioners of corrections would be willing to participate in that type of mediation setting? There was no blaming or shouting. Both were prepared by the mediator to make this session productive and helpful to all involved.

Specialized training in family mediation and victim and offender mediation can be added to the training package once the program has a track record. After a program has been established, it can be continued internally by existing personnel without additional expense. Mediation training can be part of the normal curriculum, and those who wish to be mediators can go on from the conflict-management unit to the mediation training.

How Does Mediation Work?

The Setting

In a correctional institution or in a community corrections setting, the disputing parties meet in a private conference room with the mediator(s). There should be a table and chairs with paper and small pencils. The parties with the dispute look at each other face-to-face across the table and the mediator sits between them. If there are co-mediators, the mediators should sit on opposite ends of the table so that they can face each other and see all the nonverbal expressions from the co-mediator and the participants.

Opening Statement

The mediators explain their role and thank the people for their willingness to sit down together to see if they can reach a mutual agreement.

The mediators are there to help both parties work together on the issues. The mediators are impartial and neutral. The mediators do not take sides. A trust level has to be established by the mediators for both participants. This trust level begins in the preparation stage and continues to build in the opening statement with a clear description of the role of the mediator. It has to continue throughout the mediation by keeping the dialog balanced and equal. Both sides have to feel the mediator is working to create a forum where they can talk freely and where no judgments are going to tip the scales in the other person's favor.

The mediators review the agenda and explain the process. Expectations are spelled out, such as not interrupting each other and showing each other respect by not calling each other names and staying seated. Paper and pencil can be used by the parties to write down ideas that might come up to be referred to when it is their turn to speak.

Confidentiality

To work with any credibility, the mediation process must be confidential. This is explained to the participants to get them to talk about the problem without fear of retaliation from the system. When problems arise that may need private clarification, the mediators can call for a caucus and meet with each person privately for equal periods of time and then continue the mediation. What is discussed in caucus is also confidential and is not revealed in the mediation session unless the person agrees to discuss it. If serious threats are made by one of the parties, the process can be halted. Any statement or action taken after the session has been stopped will be subject to the normal consequences. This is explained clearly to all parties. The mediators cannot be asked to testify against either party at a future court action or hearing. This may appear to be a problem in the corrections field. In the majority of the mediations, it will not pose any conflict of interest. If individual correctional professionals do not feel comfortable in this role, they should bring in a colleague to mediate.

Not every person is a candidate for mediation training. Neutrality is essential. If the participants begin to talk about matters that are not appropriate for mediation, for example, threats of violence or contraband, the mediator can explain that these issues cannot be addressed in mediation and can stop the session, if appropriate. The benefits received from mediation make the confidentiality requirement a small price to pay in the corrections field.

If the mediation results in a written agreement, the parties can have the document sent to the proper authorities for implementation. The mediators must guard the confidentiality in the mediation session closely.

The word will go around the institution quickly whether individuals can say what they want in the session and if it goes any further than the mediation room.

Dialog

The key to mediation is ensuring that all parties have the uninterrupted opportunity to express fully their position and feelings. Allowing persons to say what they want not only helps them to be heard, but it also allows them to hear the other party. Venting feelings under controlled conditions lets the parties get it off their chests so that they can work on solutions and reach an agreement.

The exchanges must be balanced between the parties so that information can be shared. Many times in a corrections setting, a power imbalance may develop. The mediator constantly must be alert to have each person talk and have equal input into the discussion. Information is power and information also is healing. With correct information, people can put their energy into solving the problem and not attacking the person.

Identify the Issues

The mediators assist the disputants in clarifying and pinpointing the real differences in the disagreement. The key points must be identified and discussed, and the needs of both parties must be seen. Just the process of talking it out often will give the parties the relief they are looking for from the other person and diffuse the issue.

Discuss the Options and Solutions

The answers to most dilemmas lie in the minds of the parties themselves. They usually can come up with the best solution. It may involve conflict-management techniques like compromise, and it certainly will include negotiation. Negotiation is talking to each other with the goal of finding terms of agreement.

If and when the parties mutually agree on a solution, they must give the solution a reality test. This involves the development of an implementation plan. This can be written with specific dates, amounts of payment (restitution), and community service, or it can be an oral commitment with or without a handshake. A handshake is up to the parties themselves and should be mutual and what they feel comfortable in doing.

Closure

In this last stage, the mediator asks the parties if there are any other final words or statements and gives each person an opportunity to make any final comments. The mediator then thanks both parties for all their good work and encourages them to look to the future and learn from the past. If the disputants encounter problems implementing the agreement, they can work them out together or return to mediation.

Mediation is a process that a correctional institution can use to address inmate complaints. Rather than tie up the legal system with numerous filed grievances, mediation could resolve a majority of these types of matters. The inmate is heard, and the institutional representative discusses the available resources, and they both look at the options and try to agree on a solution. It will help improve inmate morale and help create a less volatile atmosphere in the facility. The cost of having these matters go to court will be reduced, the institutions will save time and energy, and inmates will learn how to negotiate and solve their own problems.

If this type of process is available within the institution, the matter not only often can be heard and resolved, but the entire atmosphere of the facility has the potential to be changed for the better. The parties must be ready to negotiate in good faith. If their purpose is to create frivolous lawsuits or one or both of the parties do not agree to mediate, then more traditional litigation is necessary.

Mediation in the community has been very successful in helping people solve criminal matters and civil disputes like employer-employee problems, landlord-tenant disputes, and family issues. The probation officer and parole agent can use mediation or refer clients to a local community dispute resolution center. Such centers are available in every state and there are more than 400 programs nationwide. The service is normally free to indigents. For example, in New York, the court system sponsors dispute resolution centers in each of its sixty-two counties. Thousands of criminal, civil, and family issues are resolved each year. For further information on this statewide network, contact the Community Dispute Resolution Centers Program of the New York Unified Court System, (518) 473-4160.

Victim and Offender Mediation

One of the most powerful forms of mediation and restorative justice in the criminal justice system is the process of bringing the victim of a crime together with the person who committed the crime. This process can be employed in misdemeanor criminal cases, and it is also very effective in felony criminal cases where the victim or the victim's family needs information and answers to relieve their pain and suffering. This is a voluntary process and usually is initiated by the victim. In cases involving juveniles and first-time adult offenders, it can be offered to the victim as a better approach than the traditional adjudication process. There are more than 300 victim and offender programs in the United States, and it is being used in more than 700 programs in other countries throughout the world. Restitution has been used for generations by indigenous cultures.

The Native Americans call the process *real justice* rather than restorative justice. In a case in New York where a drive-by shooting took place on a reservation, a mediation was conducted between the Native American families of both the victim and the offender. The clan mother served as the mediator. The shooting injured the father of one of the families. He had been in the house at the time the other party drove by and shot into the house. He was hit in the leg and was not able to work. The entire matter was discussed, and the underlying problems were identified. The parties agreed on restitution for the medical expenses, and the offender completed the work the father was doing on the house under the father's supervision. When all was accomplished after one year, the criminal charges were dropped. This may be a better way to handle many criminal matters in certain situations—if both parties agree.

What are the benefits of a victim and offender mediation for the victim? Why would a person who has been a victim of a crime even want to see the other person much less sit down and talk to that person? Crime is an interaction between the victim and the perpetrator. It is a relationship that has negative consequences. With mediation and restorative justice, the parties are seeking to repair the harm done by the action of one person against another. The most effective way to begin this process is to bring the parties together to talk to each other.

If half of what is called crime is between people who already know each other, there is already a relationship. Stranger-on-stranger crime also has the beginning of a negative encounter. To resolve the negative conflict created in the lives of these people, some type of positive interaction is necessary and closure is possible. Victim and offender mediation is a voluntary process. Many times it is initiated by the victim looking for peace of mind and an end to this nightmare. The victim benefits from going through this experience by being given the opportunity to participate actively in the process of resolving the incident.

If restitution is indicated, there is the opportunity for more involvement by the victim in drawing up the restitution amount with the offender and the likelihood of collecting increases. Also, the victim becomes better informed about the incident itself. The motive, the method of operation, and the background to the event are all questions that may be important to the victim. Information is power, and the victim can be empowered with the answers to these traumatic events. The victim can deal better with fear, anger, frustration, anxiety, and a sense of alienation. If the offender is a stranger, the victim can find out who this person is.

In one mediation the author conducted in upstate New York, the victim saw the offender who shot him during a robbery as a monster. After the mediation, the victim appeared before a parole board member and recommended that the offender be released on his next parole hearing. He had served twelve years in prison for his offense. After being released, the offender also was helped by the victim in his employment search. This particular mediation was filmed by Home Box Office (HBO) and is shown periodically on television under the title "Confronting Evil."

The victim also can benefit from mediation by learning more about the criminal justice system. Rather than just being a bystander, the victim can have a real role in seeking justice in a positive manner.

The victim also is given an opportunity to resolve the incident in a constructive and thorough manner, which helps to assure a peaceful future. The victim gains peace of mind and a sense of closure, and he can let go of the incident and put it behind him. In another case this writer mediated, which was filmed by 48 Hours on CBS television, a mother met with the drunk driver who killed her twenty-two-year-old daughter in a car crash. He was serving the seventh year of a fifteen-year sentence he received after pleading guilty to vehicular homicide. The woman not only received answers to troubling questions, but she also saw who he was and was able to see his remorse and his efforts to address his alcoholism. She forgave him and wrote to the parole board recommending that he be released at his next parole date.

In serious felony cases, the victim and offender must be prepared carefully by the mediator to be ready to benefit from the process. The victim who is looking for revenge is not a candidate for mediation. Victims should want answers, information, and an opportunity for closure to put the experience behind them and to let go of the anger and the pain. Offenders must be accountable and ready to admit their involvement in the crime. Some sign of remorse must be evident.

Why should an offender participate in this type of mediation? Why not just do the time? The offender already is being punished by society so why add to the trouble? If the offenders can be interviewed and restorative justice concepts can be planted in their minds, they can begin to think about changing their behavior. By meeting with the victim, they can become aware of the harm suffered by the victims and the human costs and consequences.

The offender has an opportunity to make it right with the victim, to acknowledge responsibility, and to do whatever is possible to express remorse and make amends. In other words, the offender has a chance to restore a sense of justice. How many offenders would be willing or even want to become involved in something like this? If the information is properly explained, many offenders would jump at the chance to get it off their chest and try to repair the damage. Why not give them the opportunity to make it right? The option is to continue to do what is being done, namely, punish the offender, period. Even good parenting does not recommend only punishing the children and not educating, forgiving, and welcoming them back as full members of the family. One of this author's theories on a major cause of crime is immaturity on the part of the offender, whether it is greed in a white-collar criminal or poor choices by a youthful offender. Victim and offender mediation allows the offender to take a step toward maturity.

Another benefit for an offender who participates in mediation is the opportunity to be accountable and to take full responsibility for one's behavior. There is no excuse that washes. Choices were made and the consequences followed. In the retributive model, offenders are at an advantage to deny all guilt and try to get off. They hire or are assigned a lawyer who will speak for them. In restorative justice and mediation, the focus is on repairing the damage and speaking for yourself.

Finally, in the mediation mode, the offenders also have the opportunity to learn and become more informed about the impact of their actions, the workings of the criminal justice system, the options that are available, and what is happening and why. Through this participation, the offenders have a sense of ownership and commitment to live up to any agreement. It is an experience that will influence the offenders for the rest of their lives. Think about the choice of having every offender go through some type of mediation as opposed to just getting probation or sitting in an institution and complaining about the system that put them there.

In the upstate New York victim-and-offender mediation discussed previously, which involved an offender who shot his victim during a robbery, the offender witnessed a drive-by shooting while he was on parole in his community. He recognized the driver and the shooter. He spoke with us about what he should do. He ultimately decided to testify against the two perpetrators, and they were convicted. The parolee stated that he was not a "snitch," but, instead, was paying back the community for his own past actions. This demonstrates the power of victim and offender mediation and restorative justice.

The criminal justice system benefits from mediation because it is an alternative process for dealing with many minor cases that could be resolved without having to go through a full court procedure. It can be a cost-effective means of resolving many of these cases. It is a positive way for people to participate in and understand the workings of the criminal justice system. Victims can participate in the process and obtain answers to relieve anger and frustration at the system. The offender and the victim both can experience justice.

The community benefits because it empowers the parties to resolve their own problems and build for the future. Many community members receive training to become mediators and volunteer to help people to resolve their own conflicts in a constructive manner and avoid the situation from escalating into more serious matters. It is very cost effective when a problem can be resolved in the community and those involved do not have to travel through the justice system or into court. This process restores a sense of justice and peace to the community as a whole and the individual communities of the victim and offender.

To read more on victim and offender mediation see *Victim Meets Offender: The Impact of Restorative Justice and Mediation* by Mark S. Umbreit, Willow Tree Press, Inc., Monsey, New York, 1994.

For more information on victim and offender mediation, contact:

Greg Richardson, M.A., J.D., or Bill Preston, J.D.
Victim and Offender Mediation Association
P.O. Box 16301
Washington, DC 20041-16301
Telephone: (703) 404-1246
Fax: (703) 404-4213
E-mail: grichardjd@aol.com

Chapter VIII

Restorative Justice, Conflict Management, Conflict Resolution, and Corrections

Restoring a sense of justice to individuals and communities is a monumental task. Retributive justice, in vogue today, focuses on punishment. In this vein, crime is seen as an act of conflict against the state or federal government. It is a violation of the law. The criminal justice system controls what is done to address this type of conflict called crime. Crime is an individual act with individual responsibility. Offender accountability is defined as taking punishment. Punishment is believed to be effective in deterring crime and changing behavior. The victim is peripheral to the process.

The community, except in the limited case of serving as a juror or testifying as a witness, is on the sideline and is a spectator represented by the local, state, or federal government. The focus is on blame and guilt. There is an adversarial relationship with the government on one side and the accused on the other. Conflict arises when someone violates a law and the criminal justice system steps into the picture. The police officer arrests the person, the jailer detains, the district attorney prosecutes and, if convicted in a trial, the judge sentences, the probation officer supervises and monitors, or the correctional personnel house and manage the movement and programming of the incarcerated individual. After release, unless the full sentence is served, the parole agent has the individual under supervision and surveillance again.

Another approach to dealing with criminal acts of conflict is called restorative justice. This is the philosophy that has been emphasized in this book as a better way to manage and resolve conflict in the long run. In restorative justice, crime is seen as an act against another person and the community. The control lies primarily in the community. Accountability is defined as assuming responsibility and taking action to repair the harm. Crime has both individual and social dimensions of responsibility. Punishment is a consequence of negative behavior, but it alone is not effective in changing behavior and is disruptive to community harmony and constructive relationships. The victim is central to the process of resolving the crime. The offenders are viewed by their capacity to repair the damage due to the crime (reparation). The emphasis is on problem solving, liabilities, obligations, and on the future. Dialog and negotiation are key ingredients. Restitution is the beginning of restoring justice to the victim and the community. The community facilitates this process. The victim, offender, and the community are directly involved.

Some people may say that this is not realistic. It never will work. The only answer is to lock these people up and throw away the keys. However, getting back to being realistic, one has to admit that society has tried the punishment approach and it has resulted in crowded, costly prisons; recidivism is high, and crime and violence continue to be a major concern for people. The atmosphere between the convicted and the keepers is strained, at best.

Perhaps it is time to try a different approach. No, it does not mean close the prisons. There are dangerous people out there who cannot function in open society. These individuals need to be taken out of their communities and placed in a safe and secure community where they cannot harm themselves or others. But, these people also can practice restorative justice whether it is being in a mental hospital or serving a life term in prison. Restorative justice can be used with juveniles and adults accused or convicted of misdemeanors and felonies. The concept can be effective in the community and in the correctional setting.

How can restorative justice be a realistic approach to conflict management in the justice system? It already is.

Community Policing

Many cities across the country are instituting community policing because they believe it is a better approach than traditional law enforcement. The adversarial system often requires the police officer to arrest the person creating the conflict situation. Community policing recommends that the officer work with the neighborhood, and problem solving becomes the major goal. Arrests take place with probable cause when it is appropriate, but the officers are there primarily to be peace officers and to serve the community. Public safety is always paramount, but community policing can help prevent crime and get to the heart of the problem rather than simply result in an arrest.

It is an example of restoring peace in a neighborhood. The citizens and the police work together on the conflict situation.

Community Court and Diversion Programs

In diversion programs and community courts, the identification of the underlying problems is important, and perpetrator participation in resources available in the community becomes primary. Again, the emphasis is focusing on the person and resolving the problem rather than punishing the individual. Community service is part of the sentence and signifies that the individual is paying back the community.

Community Corrections

Community corrections is working with the person in trouble with the law in the individual's own community, again using all the available resources to assist the person and to repair the damage that was done by the criminal act either through restitution to the individual and/or the community. The emphasis is on restoring the victim, the offender, and the community rather than on surveillance and ongoing punishment. Probation and parole, along with day, evening, and residential programs, can be very effective in making the offender accountable and assisting the victim and the community if they incorporate a restorative-justice methodology.

Examples could include cases like school vandalism and community pranks. A number of football players on the local high-school team made bottle bombs and planted them around the community. Fortunately, no one was hurt. A group mediation with the players, their parents, their coaches, school representatives, and people from the community could meet and discuss the consequences and the danger of such a prank. The players could give a public apology and agree to perform a community service like cleaning the park for an entire summer. The court case could be continued until all the conditions of the mediation were meet. In this manner, the potential victims could be heard, the entire community would have benefitted from the community service, and the players would be held accountable for their actions. After one year, if all the community service had been completed, the matter could be dismissed and the young people would not have a criminal record to follow them throughout their lives.

The traditional manner of dealing with this sort of incident is for the players' parents to hire attorneys, deny the matter by pleading not guilty or plea bargain and delay as long as possible to try to minimize the damage. Which approach is better for young people and their future?

Restitution to the Individual

Restitution to a victim of a crime is a key ingredient of restorative justice. Through monetary restitution or symbolic restitution, the offender repairs and repays the victim for the damage done to property or for the pain suffered by the person. It is true in a violent crime that offenders cannot repair or restore completely the damage done by their actions. However, restitution is a sign of their remorse as are their efforts to help the victims in any way that they can.

In the case of the upstate New York robbery where the offender shot the victim, the offender could not remove the bullet from the victim. However, through the mediation, the offender was able to help the victim heal by giving him information and expressing his remorse. The victim was able to experience closure and let go of the post-traumatic stress that had haunted him over the years. That victim now helps other victims and offenders through public presentations and prison seminars.

Restitution Through Community Service

Community service in a restorative justice model is not an easy sentence or a slap on the wrist. It is a sign that the individuals realize that their actions affect not just the victim of their crime but the community as a whole. By performing community restitution, the individual is repaying the community and restoring a sense of justice. In the process, the individuals who did the crime are thinking about their behavior and what damage it has caused. If the community restitution is done in a perfunctory manner, then it serves little or no purpose. It is not a "chain-gang" mentality. That is why it is important for the probation officer to have a restorative-justice approach and see the work not as just another paper requirement to fulfill for the court but as a real opportunity to repair the damage that has been done. Many times when this author worked with probationers on community service projects, he saw the satisfaction on their faces after doing something positive for a change. It had them thinking and wanting to change their past lifestyle.

An Eye for an Eye

The biblical reference to "an eye for an eye and a tooth for a tooth," which often is used to justify punishment and revenge, actually limits and defines the aggrieved party's remedies against the offender. It is encouraging the victims to be repaid the equivalent of the damage they have suffered. The value of an eye or a tooth must be paid as reparation either monetarily or in services. It does not mean allowing the victims or society to destroy the offender's eye or tooth. As Mohandas K. Gandhi observed, an eye for an eye only makes the whole world blind.

A good example of reparation is a victim and offender mediation where the drunk driver agreed to pay monthly restitution for the educational costs of the victim's children. In another mediation in a correctional institution, the offender agreed to pay monthly for the gauze needed by the victim of a random drive-by shooting. The cost was only five dollars, but it was all the inmate could afford, and it had powerful symbolic meaning. He could not replace her damaged eye, but he could begin to help her in the best way he could.

A restorative justice advocate views the death penalty as an extreme punishment and an act of revenge. It restores nothing and continues to perpetuate violence as an answer.

Probation

The probation officers are in the best position to practice restorative justice. They are in the community with the offender, their families, and all of the community's resources. The needs of the probationer can be identified and opportunities to pay back the victim and the community abound. The offenders can be accountable directly to their own community. The more this process is used on probationers the less the likelihood is that they will go deeper into the criminal justice system.

The probation officer can use victim and offender mediation if all parties agree, or the officer could conduct a group conference with all the key people involved with the person in the criminal conflict. This is like an intervention where all the people sit down with the probationer and talk about the problem and how all can help resolve the incident. In the burglary committed by Nate Carter in the case study, a mediation could have been facilitated by the probation officer, Bill Sinclair. Nate Carter and his former employer could sit at the table with Bill Sinclair serving as a mediator. This experience would give Nate a chance to talk about his firing, and it would give the employer a chance to explain his position. Nate must be accountable for his actions and pay restitution for any items taken. To give the probationer the opportunity to be accountable may serve as a way to prevent the need to incarcerate the individual and may help the person think twice when another conflict situation arises.

Another example of when mediation and restorative justice can be used is when a school is vandalized. The traditional retributive approach would be to take the parties to court unless the lawyers negotiate a reduced plea, in which case the vandals learn only how to avoid the consequences of their actions rather than take responsibility for them. If a court appearance and conviction does take place and probation becomes the punishment with restitution as a condition, the perpetrator reluctantly would report once a month to a probation officer and try to meet the conditions of probation rather than the needs of the school community.

In a restorative justice model, the people accused of the vandalism would meet with a probation officer and a group conference would be explained. The vandals, along with their parents, school representatives, the local police, a student council person, and a school board member would sit down together and discuss the incident. The probation officer would facilitate the discussion. The reason for the act would be addressed, and each person could contribute to the dialog. The session would be confidential. An agreement on behavior and restitution would be worked out with the person(s) who had committed the act, and a payment schedule would be written up. Community restitution on the school grounds also could be part of the contract. The agreement would be signed by the accused parties, and a copy would be given to the court. A statement agreed upon by all parties could be prepared for the press to inform and educate the school and the greater community about what action was taken. After one year, if the monetary restitution were paid and the community work on the school grounds were completed, the matter could be dismissed—and there would be no criminal record to follow the young people for the rest of their lives.

Through the restorative justice process, the parties are held fully accountable, the school is repaired, and the community is involved in a constructive way. The conflict has been managed and resolved. There is closure, and people can look to the future.

Parole

The parole agent also can adopt a restorative justice approach. He can explain to each parolee assigned to his caseload that punishment in the form of restrictions on liberty was served when the individual was incarcerated. Now, the offender is on parole and will be supervised in the community, and the parole agent will assist the person in his reintegration as a productive member of society. The parolee can begin to repay the damage done to the community by working and developing positive relationships in his family, with his significant other, in his place of employment, and among his peers. The goal of the restorative justice parole agent is to work with the client and not to focus on the negative and use revocation as a hammer over the person's head. Revocation is a last resort when the person has committed a new crime or is a danger to himself or others, or when the offender is not ready to cooperate despite every effort by the parole agent.

Nate Carter's parole agent, Brenda Williams, would have a better chance to help Nate change his lifestyle if Nate learns conflict-management techniques and Brenda Williams assists him in his efforts to repay the community for his past actions. Without a goal and a direction, Nate Carter will go back to what he knows best—using drugs and engaging in irresponsible behavior.

Day and Evening Programs and Residential Centers

Restorative justice is an ideal philosophy for programs that have daily contact with their clients. All participants can have the concept of restorative justice explained to them. All individual and group meetings with offenders can be used to reinforce this approach. If the idea is to simply have the offenders get a job or go to school and stay off drugs, there is no underlying foundation or motivation for the persons to change their outlook or their lifestyle. With a restorative justice approach, each human being is valued, has a role to play, and a contribution to make in the community. Persons who have committed a crime against another individual and the community have an obligation to repair the damage done and demonstrate that they now are making every effort to be a positive member of their community.

Detention Staff and Residents

People who work in detention facilities or jails also have the opportunity to practice a restorative justice approach. If a person is confined as a sentenced offender, she may be in the institution for up to a year. This gives the staff ample time to work with the client and try to convince her that she has an obligation to repair the damage she has done through her actions and restore peace to the victim, the victim's family, and her own community. Correctional officer Gail Overland has an opportunity to work on Cindy Hughes every day for up to a year. Or, she has the hassle of avoiding her or commanding her to tow the line. Consistent, firm, restorative justice approaches have the potential to be more effective in the long run and teach Cindy how to deal with conflict rather than react negatively to it.

People who are in a detention facility waiting for bail, a court appearance, or a transfer to a state or federal correctional facility also can be influenced by a staff person who is practicing a restorative justice methodology. A conflict manager in this type of setting who practices restorative justice can create a peaceful environment that makes working conditions for other staff and residents more humane and efficient. This approach also gives some meaning to the stay in a detention facility.

One of the reasons for jails is to have persons stop their negative behavior and through this intervention look at what they are doing, think about it, and begin to change that behavior. Again, it is not just to punish the persons. If parents send children to their room or ground them, the purpose is not just to punish them but to have the children think about what they have done, say they are sorry, express remorse, and begin to work on changing that negative behavior and rejoin the family. Parents do not tell their children that they have to stay in their room for a year and a day. Sometimes, the punishment orientation of retributive justice causes the system to lose sight of the real purpose of law enforcement resources, namely to create peace and harmony in the community.

Corrections Staff and Inmates

In a correctional facility, it is all too easy for correctional professionals and other staff to say, "It's just a job" or "It's too late for most of these people (inmates) to change." Likewise, the inmates can look at their situations and merely conclude that they just should keep their noses clean and do the time, one day at a time. Many dedicated correctional professionals are in the field because they feel they can and are making a difference. Many inmates have true remorse and have the best intentions to change their behavior for the better. They participate in available programs, admit their crimes, and are accountable for what they have done. If given the opportunity, they will try to restore a sense of justice to those they have offended. These observations are based on this author's experience in a number of correctional facilities around the world.

For the inmates who are ready to address these issues, the correctional professional, in turn, must be ready with a restorative approach. For the inmates who are not ready to be accountable, the challenge is to work on them in positive ways. Do not give up on them. It is what everybody else has done, and they begin to accept it as their fate. If they have given up, it is their problem and their life. But a steady restorative-justice conflict manager can make a difference in the field of corrections.

One example of the power of restorative justice is the Victim Offender Reconciliation Program at the State Correctional Institution at Graterford, Pennsylvania. The program, which is chaired by Dr. Julia Hall, has been evaluated by victims as 100 percent successful. Offenders who have participated have been so moved by the concepts of restorative justice, their meetings with victims, and the solidarity of sharing their deeply felt remorse that they continue to meet in an "alumni" group. For further information, contact Dr. Julia Hall, chairperson, VORP of Graterford, c\o the Pennsylvania Prison Society, 2000 Spring Garden Street, Philadelphia, Pennsylvania 19130. This writer had the privilege of speaking to a group of "lifers" as this program was being instituted.

Inmate grievances have become a real headache for the administration and the legal system. Inmates have rights afforded them by the Constitution and through legislation. Rather than have an adversarial process every time a complaint or a request is made, a mediation could take place and a mutual agreement could be reached. If the grievance is a personal complaint—such as a repair of a shoe—the matter can be resolved by identifying the problem and solving it within a given amount of time. If it is a group complaint—such as a religious requirement—the representatives can sit down, negotiate, and mediate a reasonable resolution. The complaint that inmates are creating frivolous lawsuits can be reduced significantly.

Most people just want to be heard. Once problems have been identified, they normally can be resolved if both parties negotiate in good faith. The inmate goes back to the population, and the word goes out that you can get satisfaction through this process. Once again, the inmate learns how to resolve yesterday's conflicts, handle today's issues, and anticipate tomorrow's crises. Will this open the floodgates for more frivolous complaints? Until a system is set up and running efficiently, there may be some misuse of the process, but this can be corrected. This abuse may be a small price to pay if a process is created that involves the staff and inmate working together in a problem-solving venture that helps bring peace to an institution and teaches inmates conflict-management techniques.

A restorative justice approach can be very helpful to all correctional staff and to each inmate. The correctional staff who believe that a restorative-justice philosophy can make them better conflict managers will approach each situation as an opportunity to listen, learn, and influence both their "adversary" and the correctional environment as a whole. The correctional staff are working not only to secure the safety of the public, other staff, and inmates, but also to restore a sense of peace and a respect for justice for all of these people. All energy is directed in this way so negativity has no place in a restorative justice advocate. Whether it is working with other staff or an inmate, the attitude is the same. The goal is to serve justice and not just make it through another day.

The inmates—whether they are serving life or a year and a day—can focus on restoring justice to family members, the other inmates, and the correctional staff. The inmates cannot wait to be released to begin practicing restorative justice in their world. If they do not start now, they will not start later. The author expressed this idea in a state correctional facility recently, and the inmates stood as one and applauded. Given the opportunity, many inmates would endorse the concept. In working with lifers who will never get out, the idea of restoring justice by the way one treats family, staff, and other inmates allows them to do something positive rather than stuffing their feelings and going through a dull, hopeless routine. The lifer can write a letter of remorse and make it available to the victim's family. The letter can be handled through the correctional counselor upon a request for information on the offender's status by the victim or the victim's family. It is one way of bringing peace to their lives.

For more information on the concept of restorative justice contact:

American Correctional Association's Restorative Justice Committee
c/o Chair, Anne Seymour
746 9th Street, SE
Washington, DC 20003
Phone: (202) 547-1732
Fax: (202) 547-7329

The Restorative Justice Institute
P.O. Box 16301
Washington, D.C. 20041-16301
Phone: (703) 404-1246
Fax: (703) 404-4213
e-mail: grichardjd@aol.com
Co-Directors: Greg Richardson, M.A., J.D. and Bill Preston, J.D.

Dr. Mark Umbreit
The Center for Restorative Justice and Mediation
School of Social Work
University of Minnesota
386 McNeal Hall
1985 Bedford Avenue
St. Paul, Minnesota 55103
Phone: (612) 624-4923
Fax: (612) 625-4288
e-mail: ctr4rjm@che2.che.umn.edu

Kay Pranis, Restorative Justice Planner
Minnesota Department of Corrections
1450 Energy Park Drive, Suite 200
St. Paul, Minnesota 55108-5219
Phone: (610) 642-0329
Fax: (612) 642-0457

John Gorczyk, Commissioner
Vermont Department of Corrections
103 South Main Street
Waterbury, Vermont 05671-1001
Phone: (802) 241-2442
Fax: (802) 241-2565

For additional reading on restorative justice refer to: American Correctional Association's chapter on restorative justice (pages 357–377) in *Best Practices: Excellence in Corrections*, edited by Edward Rhine (Lanham, Maryland, American Correctional Association, 1998); *Changing Lenses*, by Howard Zehr (Scottsdale, Pennsylvania: Herald Press, 1990); *Restorative Justice: International Perspectives*, edited by Burt Galaway and Joe Hudson (Monsey, New York: Criminal Justice Press, 1996).

Chapter IX

Conclusions

Conflict is Normal

It is okay to have different perceptions on various issues. It is what makes life interesting and gives us opportunities to learn. It is what one does about conflict that is important. The effort should be on addressing the problem and not attacking the person. The most common ways of dealing with conflict in society involve doing nothing—avoidance (flight)—or competing with the person—confrontation (fight). These methods can be effective in given circumstances, but they usually are the worst ways of dealing with conflict. The best way to deal with conflict is to look for ways to work together (collaborate) on the problem and cooperate with the possibility of reaching a mutually beneficial solution.

In Corrections, Conflict Is All Pervasive

People in trouble with the law are usually in those circumstances because they did not handle conflict well. The staff—including jailers, probation officers, community-based corrections program people, correctional institutional personnel, and parole agents—have to work with people who have multiple problems and often do not manage conflict well. The correctional professional also is faced with many approaches to working in the field. It ranges from locking them up and throwing away the key to rehabilitating everyone and never giving up on anyone. The challenges for the correctional professional are to have a philosophy of working with people and to continue learning how to be more effective on the job. The correctional professional who can manage conflict and resolve it in the most constructive manner possible serves as a role model to the other staff and the clients. The more lasting challenge is to teach clients how to manage and resolve conflict in their own lives so that they can apply these skills both while they are under supervision and in their own relationships with family, friends, coworkers, and employers. The opportunity to reach the person in trouble with the law is never going to be better for the corrections field than when they have individuals under their supervision.

Conflict Management and Conflict Resolution Tools

There are a number of tools that a correctional professional can learn to use to be effective in managing and often resolving conflict situations. They are avoidance, accommodation, compromise, confrontation, cooperation, and collaboration. All these approaches can be effective in particular circumstances, but the best approach is to have cooperation and collaboration as your basic method of managing conflict. Through negotiation, communication, information exchange, and mediation, problems can be identified, solutions can be discussed, and resolutions can be found.

TALK

A handy formula for conflict management can be narrowed down to one word: TALK (Teach each other And Listen to each other and share information and Knowledge). When a conflict arises, manage the situation rather than just react to it. Listen to the person who has the problem and learn what the conflict involves. The person, in turn, listens to the correctional professional and through a cooperative and collaborative conflict-management methodology the conflict is addressed. Empathy is the cornerstone on which conflict resolution is built. Understanding can be achieved by looking at an issue from another person's perspective.

   If this approach is not effective, then the correctional professionals should reach into their toolbox and use the next best conflict-management approach for the particular problem. Correctional professionals who use cooperation and collaboration as their primary conflict-management tool not only will be effective workers, but they also will be building a better working environment and a more harmonious community.

Restoring Justice and Building a Sense of Community

The key for the correctional professional is to use the tools to manage and resolve conflict to build a sense of community among the staff and inmates, probationers, or parolees. Just as community policing helps citizens to solve problems and to improve their neighborhoods, correctional professionals can use the same concepts to restore a sense of justice and community in their workplace.

Retributive justice is negative, emphasizes punishment, and does not change anything or anyone. It perpetuates the status quo. Restorative justice makes people accountable and centers on repairing the harm done by the negative behavior.

Manipulation

The correctional professionals who have the proper conflict-management tools and a constructive attitude will deal with attempts at manipulation just as they deal with any other interpersonal problem. Manipulation is not to be feared, it is to be managed.

Time and Respect

Correctional professionals who are properly trained in conflict management and conflict resolution will make more efficient and effective use of their time and gain the respect of coworkers and clients. These people will be creating a better working and living environment for the present and the future.

Mediation

In appropriate situations, mediation can be a powerful conflict-resolution process for the corrections field. Having the people in dispute sit down and talk together about the problem with a trained mediator not only can help the people resolve the problem, but it can have a win-win reward for all involved. It can be used for inmate-inmate conflicts, staff-staff differences, and staff-inmate problems, as well as with employer-employee problems, landlord-tenant squabbles, family issues, and in restitution cases with juvenile delinquents and adult probationers and parolees. Mediation also can restore a sense of justice in victim-and-offender matters from misdemeanors to serious felonies.

The Case Studies

In the case study of Nathaniel "Nate" Carter, there were many opportunities for correctional professionals to employ conflict-management and conflict-resolution techniques. Here is a quick review:

- Mediate Nate's employment problem with the employer before he fires Nate or even after he is fired to see if he can salvage the job.
- Mediate the burglary with the employer and Nate, with restitution and community service as the sentence rather than a prison term.
- Mediate the earlier school problems with teachers and peers.
- Conduct an intervention to address Nate's drinking and substance abuse.
- Conduct a parent-child mediation with Nate and his parents.
- Have Nate attend a program for batterers and refer his girlfriend, Tina Lopez, to a program for victims of domestic violence.
- Have Nate attend conflict-management seminars while on probation, during incarceration, or while on parole.

In the case study of Cynthia Leslie Hughes, the opportunities also were available for the correctional professional to use conflict-management techniques rather than traditional approaches. For example:

- Have a parent\teenager mediation between Cindy and her daughter, Lily, to work on parenting and teenage issues.
- Have a victim and offender mediation between Cindy and the victims of her bad-check writing and draw up a realistic restitution schedule.
- Have a mediation between Cindy and correctional officer Gail Overland over the confrontation in the cellblock.
- Have a mediation with the police and Cindy over the accusations of racism.

Correctional professionals teaching both Nate and Cindy conflict-management and conflict-resolution techniques can have a major influence on their future in the justice system.

Implementing Conflict Management and Conflict Resolution Techniques with a Restorative Justice Approach

The ideas on managing conflict and resolving conflicts can be implemented with a restorative-justice approach on two different levels. Individual professionals in the criminal justice system can adopt this style because it makes sense and appeals to them. People of this mode can read about these concepts and take courses on conflict management and mediation. In every state, there are dispute-resolution programs providing mediation training. Many criminal justice professionals are volunteering to serve as community mediators. They then can bring these skills to their personal lives and their employment.

The second level involves leadership on the state and local level. Departments of corrections and probation and parole offices can make conflict management, conflict resolution, and restorative justice a priority and require it in their basic training for all personnel. There are a number of states, such as Minnesota, Ohio, and Vermont that have a restorative justice planning unit. Local probation offices also are instituting restorative justice approaches and using victim and offender mediation on both the juvenile and adult levels, particularly for restitution cases.

Trainers are available from local community dispute resolution centers to teach conflict management and conflict resolution through mediation. In New York, for example, the Unified Court System has thirty-six certified mediation trainers across the state. Organizations like the American Arbitration Association and the Better Business Bureau provide this type of training. Many community colleges, universities, law schools, and business colleges now have courses on dispute resolution. Correctional professionals in charge of training areas can receive basic training in conflict management and then adapt it to their special needs. All staff should be trained on all levels in conflict management. Those staff who express interest should be trained in conflict resolution with mediation as the major process. Once staff have been trained, then probationers, inmates, and parolees should be given seminars and training in conflict management.

Again, those inmates who express interest should be trained in mediation to handle inmate-inmate disputes and comediate with a trained staff mediator in staff-inmate disputes. When the correctional institution has problems that affect the entire population, for example, religious requirements, the inmate mediators can be available to assist the administration in resolving the differences and reaching a mutually agreeable solution. Conflict-management and conflict-resolution techniques are available and can be a powerful force in the corrections field.

Epilog

Conflict Management and Conflict Resolution in Corrections

This work has been an effort to take a critical look at conflict in the field of corrections. It is not enough to look at conflict-management techniques and try to apply them to conflict situations in a correctional environment. One must have a philosophy of life and a psychology of working with people in trouble with the law. If criminal justice professionals see their job as a path to fulfillment in life and use a restorative approach to accomplish this goal, they can be constructive members of the justice team. If people feel that their job is simply to arrest, detain, prosecute, defend, sentence, revoke, incarcerate, monitor, or maintain, then the present system will continue and little progress will be made. Conflict will be managed or not managed for each given situation; some problems will be resolved temporarily or not resolved at all. People will go from one conflict situation to another. Little will change.

For those of you who see value in restorative justice, this total approach to conflict management can be a model that can be applied in every interaction. There will be times when one has to confront a situation and fair and firm action is the best solution. Once order has been restored, the principles of cooperation and collaboration can be applied and the parties in conflict may begin again to learn how to manage their own conflict better. Lack of cooperation did not work; the individuals can learn from that and not have to worry that their past actions will determine that the only approach that works with these persons is confrontation. Some people—both staff and client—take longer to get the message than others. Some people have learned the wrong techniques, and it takes a while to learn new behaviors. But avoidance, confrontation, and competition teach more of the same.

For those of you who cannot quite buy all the principles of restorative justice but see some value in the general approach to conflict management and conflict resolution, use the techniques and keep your mind open. Treat each person as you would want to be treated.

For those of you who do not believe any of these ideas have much merit and do not think they would work for you, keep an open mind if you want your environment to change for the better. If your coworker is negative, encourage him or her to have an open mind. If your coworkers are trying to manage and resolve conflict and use cooperative and collaborative approaches, watch how it works for them. It will not threaten your security. Use what works for you and keep your eyes open. As staff and clients use these techniques, more will be changed than just the day-to-day routine. Effective techniques to manage conflict situations and resolve problems will make your work environment and your life better. Use effective conflict-management and conflict-resolution tools to help build a workable and livable corrections community.

About the Author

Thomas Frank Christian comes from three generations of criminal justice professionals. He brings his own thirty-five years of experience to this book. He has worked in correctional and detention facilities and was a senior probation officer. He has run an award-winning community-based residential corrections program that just celebrated its twenty-fifth anniversary. He was the State Director of the Minnesota International Halfway House Association and one of the founders and first State Director of the Minnesota Community Corrections Association. In 1979, he was voted the Minnesota Corrections Person of the Year and given their Professional Achievement Award. He has worked in a number of states providing training and technical assistance.

He recently has retired after serving for fifteen years as the State Director of the Community Dispute Resolution Centers Program for the New York Unified Court System. He directed the development of community justice centers in all sixty-two New York counties. More than 25,000 conciliations, mediations, and arbitrations in family, civil, and criminal areas are handled each year by these programs and diverted from the court system. In 1997, he was awarded the Peace Builder Award by the New York State Dispute Resolution Association.

Dr. Christian has mediated a number of serious criminal matters between the victim, the victim's family, and the offender. His mediations have appeared on CBS' *48 Hours*, Home Box Office (HBO), and National Public Radio. He presently does training for people interested in victim and offender mediation.

He has a master's degree in criminal justice and a doctorate in social science from the Michigan State University School of Criminal Justice. He lives in Tucson, Arizona, with his wife. He is the father of three grown children.